Business Entry: Starting vs Buying

Essential Knowledge for Smart Business Decisions

A Practical Guide to Evaluating and Valuing Your Business Options

CHARLIE VICTOR

Impisi™

Impisi™ Media LLC
Small Business Series

Business Entry: Starting vs Buying

A Practical Guide to Evaluating and Valuing Your Business Options

CHARLIE VICTOR

Impisi™Media LLC

Business Entry Starting vs Buying - Essential Knowledge for Smart Business Decisions

ISBN: 978-1-965722-05-3 (eBook)
ISBN: 978-1-965722-06-0 (Paperback)

The case studies in this book are based on real-life experiences. To protect privacy, names, locations, and identifying details have been changed or omitted. Any resemblance to persons, businesses, or places beyond the intended examples is coincidental. The lessons and Insights are genuine and provide practical guidance to readers on their entrepreneurial journey.

Book design by Ciska Venter.

First printing edition 2024.

Published by Impisi™ Media LLC in the United States of America.
5830 E 2ND ST, STE 7000, CASPER, WY 82609
+1 (307) 275 8745
www.impisimedia.com
Impisi™ is subject to a trademark application by Impisi Media LLC.

Contents

Also by the Publisher

Small Business Series

Should You Start a Business or Not?
Business Entry: Starting vs Buying
3 Keys to Maximize Profit

Smart Work-Life Series

Mastering Time for Productivity
The Wolf's Edge

Click or scan the QR code to receive updates on new
releases and book resources.

"The only limit to our realization of tomorrow is our doubts of today" – *Franklin D. Roosevelt*

This quote encourages us to push beyond self-imposed limitations. Our future potential is bound only by the doubts we allow today. By overcoming uncertainty, we open the door to greater possibilities and success.

Introduction

"It's not about ideas. It's about making ideas happen" –
Scott Belsky

Purpose of the Book

This book aims to equip prospective entrepreneurs with the tools and knowledge to make informed decisions when entering the world of business. Whether you are considering starting a business from scratch or buying an existing one, this guide offers a comprehensive comparison of both options.

Many people believe that starting a business is the only path to entrepreneurship, but that isn't always the case. Buying a business can offer several advantages, such as an existing customer base and established operations. By understanding both routes, you can decide which aligns best with your goals, skills, and risk tolerance.

Entrepreneurship is a significant commitment, and the decisions you make early on can set the course for success or failure. This book addresses the most critical factors you must consider before taking the leap. Starting from the basics, we will explore the advantages and disadvantages of each approach. Additionally, we'll dive into practical strategies to ensure that whichever route you choose, it's backed by solid research, preparation, and a clear understanding of what lies ahead.

The purpose of this book is not just to present information but to offer actionable advice. We have designed each chapter to walk you through decision-making frameworks, give real-life examples, and suggest actionable steps. For example, if you're leaning towards starting a business, you'll find detailed guidance on creating business plans, setting up operations, and launching effectively. If buying a business seems more appealing, you will find step-by-step instructions on valuing businesses, conducting due diligence, and negotiating the purchase. In both cases, our goal is to help you avoid the common pitfalls that trip up many first-time entrepreneurs.

Ultimately, this book is about empowering you to take control of your business journey. With the insights and practical advice offered here, you will be able to navigate the complexities of entrepreneurship more confidently. Whether you choose to start fresh or build on an existing foundation, the decision is yours—and this guide will help ensure you make the best choice for your future.

How to Use This Book

This book is designed to be a practical guide that you can refer to throughout your business journey. Whether you are starting from scratch or evaluating an existing business to buy, you can follow the structured chapters to guide your decision-making process. The goal is to provide you with actionable steps at every stage. Each chapter builds on the previous one, so it is beneficial to read the book sequentially. However, you may also skip specific sections if you are looking for targeted advice.

Each chapter concludes with a recap and an action plan. These sections serve as checklists, reminding you of the key points covered and offering concrete steps for implementation. For example, after reading about the pros and cons of starting a business, you will find actionable items that help you assess whether starting a new venture is the right choice for you. This ensures that you are not just absorbing information but also applying it to your unique situation.

The book also includes case studies and real-life examples that you can use to compare your circumstances. These examples span various industries and types of businesses, giving you a broader perspective. Whether you are looking to start a tech startup, buy a retail store, or invest in a franchise, the practical insights will help you avoid common mistakes and learn from others' experiences.

In addition to the main content, the appendices provide valuable tools and references. **Appendix A** collates all the action plans from each chapter into a comprehensive checklist that can guide your decision-making process from start to finish. **Appendix B** offers a list of resources, including video links, documents, and spreadsheets that will aid you in your business journey. **Appendix C** is a glossary of key terms, ensuring you understand any unfamiliar terminology throughout the book. These appendices are designed to enhance your learning experience and provide quick reference points as you move through your business entry process.

Recap of key concepts from Book 1

In *Book 1: Should I Start a Business*, we explored foundational concepts that are essential for prospective entrepreneurs to understand before venturing into business. The book aimed to demystify entrepreneurship by providing clear, actionable guidance on the processes of starting and managing a business.

We began by discussing **reasons to start a business**. These ranged from the desire for independence to financial goals and lifestyle choices. Independence, for many entrepreneurs, is the freedom to control their time and decisions, while financial goals include achieving profitability, wealth, or financial security. Additionally, lifestyle choices, such as work-life balance, motivated some entrepreneurs to prioritize their personal goals through business ownership.

Key business components were also explored in detail. These include capital, labor, technology, profit margins, product attributes, and market phenomena. Each of these components plays a significant role in how a business works and grows. Understanding these components helps entrepreneurs make informed decisions about their business model, whether it involves managing capital intensity, staying current with technology, or setting competitive profit margins.

In *Book 1*, we also delved into the **types of businesses** that entrepreneurs can start, focusing on their legal structures and core business sectors. We examined sole proprietorships, partnerships, limited liability companies (LLCs), and corporations, each offering different levels of liability protection and administrative complexity.

Entrepreneurs were encouraged to choose the structure that aligns with their goals, resources, and risk tolerance. In addition to legal structures, the book explored various sectors such as retail, service, and manufacturing, highlighting how each sector operates and the unique challenges and opportunities they present. This understanding of business types helps entrepreneurs make informed choices about the legal and operational framework that best suits their vision.

Lastly, the book emphasizes the importance of **continuous learning and adaptation**. Entrepreneurship is not static, and as the business environment changes, successful entrepreneurs must be willing to evolve. The ability to adapt to new market trends, technological advances, and customer needs is critical for long-term success.

This book offers exclusive downloadable resources, detailed in the Appendices. These can be accessed by scanning or clicking the QR code, or link. Alternatively, you can download them directly from our website at www.impisimedia.com/resources, simply use the password **SBSB2**

Chapter 1
Understanding Your Options

"Panic causes tunnel vision. Calm acceptance of danger allows us to more easily assess the situation and see the options" – Simon Sinek

Overview of Business Entry Methods

Choosing the best way to enter the business world depends on your resources, goals, and tolerance for risk.

Starting a business offers control and the chance to build something unique. It allows you to create a brand, develop a product, and shape the company culture from scratch. However, the risks are high. New businesses face significant hurdles, including financial losses, market uncertainty, and the challenge of building a customer base. The success rate for startups is lower than that of established businesses, which adds to the stress of starting fresh.

On the other hand, buying an existing business provides immediate access to established customers, systems, and cash flow. The primary advantage is that much of the legwork, like market research and branding, has already been done. Yet, buying a business can be costly upfront, and you may inherit hidden problems like outdated practices or unhappy employees. Proper due diligence is key to making this option work. Additionally, you might have less flexibility to make changes, as the existing customer base may expect continuity.

Franchising offers another route, combining the support of a proven system with the independence of running a business. Franchises benefit from brand recognition and operational support. However, the downside is the lack of full control. Franchisees must follow strict guidelines, and there are ongoing fees that can reduce profitability.

Synergies can occur when you start a business and later buy existing ones to expand. This strategy offers flexibility, helping entrepreneurs blend creativity with stability. Partnerships and intrapreneurship also offer appealing alternatives. Partnerships allow shared risk and resources, while intrapreneurship lets you innovate within an existing company.

To conclude this chapter, we will discuss entry costs, risk tolerance, and emotional factors, as these are crucial in deciding the best path for you.

Starting a Business

Pros of Starting a Business

Starting a business from scratch gives you complete control over every aspect of the venture. You have the freedom to develop your vision and turn it into reality.

This control extends to your brand identity, company culture, and product or service offerings. You can build your business around your values and your desired customer experience. Moreover, starting your own business allows you to innovate and differentiate yourself from competitors. When you begin with a clean slate, there are no constraints, allowing for creative freedom in your approach.

Another advantage is the potential for higher rewards. Since you are the sole creator of the business, the profits generated belong entirely to you. This autonomy can be incredibly rewarding, both financially and emotionally. Building a successful business from the ground up can provide immense personal satisfaction, knowing that you created something from nothing.

Additionally, starting your business can be more affordable initially compared to buying an established one. You have control over costs and can start small, expanding only when it makes sense. Many startups begin as lean operations, giving the entrepreneur the ability to grow at a comfortable pace.

Cons of Starting a Business

Starting a business also comes with significant challenges. The most considerable downside is the financial risk. New businesses need capital, and there is no guarantee that your efforts will yield profits. In the initial stages, many businesses operate at a loss while trying to build a customer base and establish a market presence. This can be stressful, especially if personal savings or loans are involved.

Another con is the steep learning curve. Entrepreneurs must wear many hats, from marketing and operations to accounting and human resources. It can be overwhelming to manage everything, particularly without prior experience in these areas. Additionally, the time commitment is immense. Starting a business often requires long hours, leaving little room for personal life. The pressure to succeed can be emotionally taxing, and failure rates are high for startups, which adds to the stress.

Market uncertainty is another risk. You must create demand for your product or service, which can be difficult, especially in competitive or saturated markets. There's also the unpredictability of customer behavior, which can affect your business's performance and growth.

Throughout this book, we will further explore these pros and cons, focusing on how they affect entry costs, risk tolerance, and emotional factors.

Buying an Existing Business

Pros of Buying an Existing Business

Buying an existing business can offer several advantages over starting one from scratch. One of the most significant benefits is that the business is already established. This means there is a proven track record of revenue, customers, and market presence. You can bypass many of the struggles that startups face, such as building a brand, developing customer loyalty, and creating operational systems. Additionally, an existing business usually comes with trained staff who understand the daily operations, which can help you transition smoothly into ownership.

Another benefit is immediate cash flow. When you buy an existing business, you can start generating income right away, assuming the business is profitable. This is a stark contrast to starting a business, which often requires months or even years to become financially sustainable. The infrastructure, supply chain, and relationships with suppliers and customers are already in place, allowing you to focus on growth and improvement rather than initial setup.

Furthermore, obtaining financing can sometimes be easier when buying an established business. Lenders may view an existing business with historical financial data as a lower risk compared to a new venture with no history. This makes it more likely to secure loans or attract investors, especially if the business has a history of profitability.

Cons of Buying an Existing Business

While buying a business comes with clear advantages, it also carries some potential downsides. The upfront cost is usually much higher than starting a new business. You are not only paying for the tangible assets, like equipment and inventory, but also for the intangible assets, such as goodwill, brand reputation, and customer relationships. This can make buying a business expensive, and the return on investment might take longer than expected.

Another risk is inheriting problems. No business is perfect, and when you buy one, you could be taking on hidden issues. These may include outdated systems, unmotivated staff, or even legal liabilities. Proper due diligence is essential, but even with thorough investigation, some challenges may not become clear until you are fully involved in the operations.

Finally, there is often less flexibility when you buy an established business. The existing customer base may have certain expectations, and changing key aspects of the business could alienate them. You may also have to deal with the previous owner's reputation, for better or worse, which can affect your ability to innovate and grow.

In this book, we will explore buying a business in more detail, along with discussions on costs, risk, and valuation.

Buying a Franchise

When buying a franchise, there are two distinct routes: buying a franchise that is already operational or buying into a franchise where you will need to start operations from scratch at a new location. Both options fall under the franchise model but present unique challenges and opportunities. Buying a franchise is different from starting an independent business because you are purchasing the rights to operate under an existing brand with a proven business model. Whether you buy an existing franchise or start a new one, you gain access to an established network of support, but your level of control and potential risks can vary greatly.

Pros of Buying a Franchise

One of the main advantages of buying a franchise is the opportunity to operate under a well-known brand. Franchises offer the benefit of brand recognition, which can provide immediate customer trust and loyalty. When you buy a franchise, especially one that is already up and running, you may also gain an established customer base, allowing you to start generating revenue quickly. Even in the case of a new franchise location, the brand's reputation can help attract customers faster than if you were building a business from the ground up.

Additionally, franchises provide comprehensive support and guidance. Most franchisors offer training programs, marketing support, and operational systems to help franchisees succeed. This structure reduces the risks involved with starting a business since you are working within a proven model. For those without much business experience, this level of support can be particularly valuable.

Financing can also be more accessible when buying a franchise. Banks and other lenders are often more willing to extend loans to franchisees because they are considered lower-risk investments compared to independent startups. The franchise's established success reduces uncertainty, making it easier to secure funding.

Cons of Buying a Franchise

However, buying a franchise does come with downsides. One of the main drawbacks is the cost. Franchises typically require a significant upfront investment, including franchise fees and potential royalties. In addition to this, you may have to invest in equipment, inventory, or other operational needs. These startup costs can be substantial, and it may take time before you see a return on your investment.

Another disadvantage is the lack of control. Franchisees must operate within the guidelines set by the franchisor, which can limit your ability to innovate or make changes to the business model. This lack of flexibility may frustrate entrepreneurs who want to exercise creativity and independence. Franchisors often dictate decisions related to products, pricing, and marketing, leaving little room for personal input.

Finally, you may inherit issues if you are buying an existing franchise. While the business might appear successful on the surface, there could be hidden operational or management problems that require attention. Proper due diligence is essential to ensure you are aware of any potential challenges before committing to the purchase.

In this book, we will dive deeper into starting or buying a franchise, looking closely at financial, operational, and emotional factors to help you decide if this is the right business entry choice for you.

Exploring Synergies: Expansion Through Acquisition

One effective growth strategy in business is starting a new venture and then expanding through the acquisition of existing businesses. This model allows entrepreneurs to build a solid foundation with their own startup and then scale faster by buying established businesses that complement their original operations.

Instead of growing organically at a slower pace, buying businesses offers a shortcut to rapid expansion. This strategy can be particularly useful in competitive industries where gaining market share quickly is crucial.

The combination of internal growth through your startup and external growth through acquisitions creates synergies that can lead to greater efficiency, innovation, and market presence.

Expansion through acquisition offers flexibility and strategic advantages. You can target businesses that align with your goals or fill gaps in your operations, such as buying a company with a strong distribution network or a loyal customer base.

This method allows for diversification, mitigating risks by expanding into new markets or offering more products. It also provides the opportunity to absorb competitors or suppliers, strengthening your position in the industry.

Pros of Expansion Through Acquisition

One of the biggest advantages of this strategy is speed. Starting a new business requires time to develop products, build a brand, and establish customer loyalty. Acquiring an existing business allows you to skip these initial stages and immediately benefit from established revenue streams, customers, and systems. This can be particularly helpful in industries with high barriers to entry, where developing these assets from scratch can be costly and time-consuming.

Additionally, acquisition offers opportunities for operational efficiency. When you buy a business, you may find ways to integrate its processes into your existing operation. This can lead to cost savings through economies of scale, such as combining back-office functions or negotiating better deals with suppliers due to increased buying power. Furthermore, acquisitions can strengthen your brand by absorbing a company with a good reputation or unique product offerings that complement your own.

Another benefit is diversification. Acquiring businesses in related fields or new markets helps spread risk. If one market faces difficulties, your overall business can still thrive in other areas. This diversification can stabilize your income and reduce the impact of market fluctuations.

Cons of Expansion Through Acquisition

However, expansion through acquisition is not without its challenges. One major drawback is the upfront cost. Buying an existing business is usually expensive, as you're buying not only its assets but also its goodwill, customer base, and market share. Financing these acquisitions can put significant pressure on your business, especially if you're also managing the growth of your original startup.

There's also the risk of inheriting problems. No matter how thorough your due diligence, unforeseen issues like poor management, outdated systems, or hidden liabilities may arise after the acquisition. These problems can be costly to resolve and may slow down your overall growth. Additionally, merging the culture and operations of two businesses can create friction, especially if employees are resistant to change.

Another potential issue is a lack of flexibility. Once you've acquired an existing business, it may not be as easy to innovate or pivot as it would be with your original startup. Established businesses often come with ingrained processes and customer expectations, which can limit your ability to make changes without alienating your new customer base.

Partnership and Intrapreneurship

When considering entry options into the business world, partnerships and intrapreneurship provide distinct pathways for entrepreneurs. Both offer unique advantages and challenges and should be carefully evaluated based on your goals and risk tolerance. These approaches appeal to individuals who either want to share the entrepreneurial burden or innovate within the safety of an established organization.

Partnership

A partnership is more than just a collaboration between two or more individuals; it is a legal structure that defines the relationship and responsibilities of each partner. In the UK, a partnership can take the form of a general partnership or a limited liability partnership (LLP). In Canada, partnerships are classified as general, limited, or limited liability partnerships. In the U.S., partnerships can also be structured as general partnerships or as limited liability companies (LLCs), which protect the personal assets of the partners.

The partnership decision is not restricted to starting a business from scratch. It is equally applicable when buying an existing business. The key point is that this structure allows partners to pool resources, share risks, and combine their expertise. A partnership can reduce the individual financial burden by splitting costs and risks among the partners. Additionally, it allows for complementary skill sets to be brought together, making the business more well-rounded. For example, one partner might be strong in operations while the other excels in sales or marketing.

However, partnerships come with potential challenges. Shared decision-making can lead to disagreements, which, if not effectively managed, could affect the business. Additionally, each partner may be held liable for the actions of the other, particularly in general partnerships. The success of a partnership largely depends on clear communication, defined roles, and shared vision.

Intrapreneurship

Intrapreneurship, the concept of acting like an entrepreneur within a larger company, originated in the late 1970s and was popularized in 1985 by Gifford Pinchot in his book *Intrapreneuring*. Pinchot described intrapreneurs as individuals who take initiative and drive innovation within a corporate environment, using the company's resources to create new business ventures. The term gained traction as businesses recognized the value of fostering an enterprising spirit among their employees while maintaining the security and stability of an established organization.

This model provides a low-risk option for those who want to experience entrepreneurship but without the financial and operational burdens that come with starting or buying a business.

The primary benefit of intrapreneurship is the ability to leverage the resources and security of an established company. You have access to the company's funding, expertise, and customer base, which can significantly reduce the risks associated with entrepreneurial ventures. Furthermore, the company typically provides a safety net in terms of salary and benefits, reducing personal financial risk.

However, the downside of intrapreneurship is that it often comes with less autonomy. As an intrapreneur, you still report to management and must operate within the company's broader goals and vision. This can limit your freedom to make significant changes or take bold risks. Intrapreneurship is particularly well-suited to individuals who want to innovate but prefer the stability of an existing corporate structure. It's ideal for those who are entrepreneurial in spirit but not ready or willing to take on the risks of full business ownership.

Entry Costs

When deciding on how to enter the business world, one of the most critical factors to consider is the entry cost. Entry costs vary greatly depending on whether you start a business from scratch or buy an existing one, the industry, and the size of the business.

These costs include everything from initial set-up expenses to ongoing operational costs until the business becomes profitable. It's crucial to understand that entry costs will not only affect your financial resources but also impact your time and ability to reach profitability.

Costs are influenced by the type of business model you choose. For example, starting a new business can often have lower initial costs but might take longer to become profitable. On the other hand, buying an existing business may involve higher upfront expenses, but with established customers and operations, it could generate income sooner.

In either case, entry costs include securing physical or digital infrastructure, hiring employees, and developing or acquiring products. Below are three examples of different business entry costs, varying in scale from low to high.

Low Entry Cost Example

Entry: Start

Core Industry: Freelance digital services

Type of Business: Graphic design and social media management

Typical Infrastructure Needs: Minimal. A computer, software subscriptions, and an internet connection are essential. You may also need a small budget for advertising.

Typical HR Needs: None initially, as the business can be a sole proprietorship. However, you may hire contractors or freelancers for specific tasks as the business grows.

Typical Time to Profitability and Capital Requirement: Profitability could be achieved within three to six months, depending on client acquisition speed. Initial capital requirements are low, mostly covering hardware, software, and marketing, in the range of a few thousand dollars.

Medium Entry Cost Example

Entry: Buy

Core Industry: Hospitality

Type of Business: Small café

Typical Infrastructure Needs: A leased space with kitchen equipment, tables, chairs, and permits for food service. Renovations may be needed if the space is outdated.

Typical HR Needs: A small team of staff, including baristas, servers, and a manager. Part-time or full-time employees may be needed depending on business hours.

Typical Time to Profitability and Capital Requirement: Profitability can take 12 to 24 months. Initial capital requirements include buying the café, securing the location, and covering early operational costs. Depending on the location and size, costs could range from tens of thousands to over a hundred thousand dollars.

High Entry Cost Example

Entry: Buy

Core Industry: Manufacturing

Type of Business: Mid-sized consumer goods manufacturer

Typical Infrastructure Needs: A factory or production facility, machinery, supply chain agreements, and inventory management systems. A large workspace with specialized equipment is essential.

Typical HR Needs: A large team, including production line workers, management, and logistics personnel. More support for sales, marketing, and distribution will also be needed.

Typical Time to Profitability and Capital Requirement: Profitability could take several years, depending on production efficiency and market conditions. Initial capital requirements are substantial, often reaching millions of dollars, due to equipment, staffing, and regulatory compliance.

These examples illustrate the broad spectrum of entry costs across industries and business types, highlighting how startup or acquisition strategies significantly affect the scale of investment and time to profitability.

Risk Tolerance and Comparison

Risk tolerance refers to your ability and willingness to manage uncertainty, especially in financial investments or business ventures.

In the context of business entry, it plays a critical role in determining how comfortable you are with potential losses, fluctuations, or setbacks. Your financial situation, business experience, and overall confidence in managing uncertainty influence your level of risk tolerance.

A high risk tolerance means you are more willing to accept potential losses for the chance of higher returns. In contrast, a low risk tolerance indicates a preference for more stable, predictable outcomes.

Risk tolerance can be measured both qualitatively and quantitatively. Qualitatively, you can assess it through personal reflection on how you manage stressful situations and financial uncertainty. For example, can you stay calm during market downturns or business challenges? Quantitatively, it is measured using tools like financial assessments or risk tolerance questionnaires. These tools evaluate factors such as your net worth, income stability, and financial goals, giving you a clearer understanding of how much risk you can take.

The relationship between risk and return is essential to understanding risk tolerance. The general principle in business is that higher risks often come with the potential for higher rewards. Starting a new business, for example, may involve more risk due to factors like market demand or customer acquisition challenges. However, the potential reward can be substantial if the business succeeds. Conversely, buying an established business or franchise typically involves lower risk but also lower returns, as the growth potential may already be limited by the current structure.

To illustrate the concept of risk/return, imagine you invest $100,000 to start a business. If the risk is high, you might expect a return of $200,000 or more, which reflects the possible high reward for the risk. In a lower-risk scenario, such as buying a stable franchise, your return might be $120,000, offering more security but less potential upside. In this way, you can evaluate whether the potential return justifies the risk.

When considering entry options, your risk tolerance should guide whether you start a new business, buy an existing one, or invest in a franchise. If you have a high tolerance for risk and aim for substantial returns, starting your own business might be the best choice.

If you prefer stability, buying a franchise or existing business can provide safer, more predictable returns. Understanding and aligning your risk tolerance with your entry decision is crucial for making strategic business choices.

Emotional Considerations

When deciding how to enter the business world, emotional considerations are often just as important as financial and operational factors.

Emotional considerations refer to the internal feelings, stress levels, and personal motivations that can impact your decision-making process. Starting a business, buying an existing one, or buying a franchise involves more than just numbers on a page—it can be a deeply personal journey that tests your emotions and resilience. Understanding the emotional toll of entrepreneurship is crucial for making a decision that aligns with both your mental and emotional well-being.

For some, the excitement of starting a business from scratch can bring immense satisfaction and fulfillment. The ability to create something entirely new from the ground up appeals to those who enjoy taking risks and have a high tolerance for uncertainty. However, this path also brings significant stress, particularly in the initial stages when long hours, financial strain, and unpredictability can weigh heavily on an entrepreneur. Others might find the pressure overwhelming, preferring a more structured and stable entry into business.

Personality type plays a significant role in how individuals respond to these emotional challenges. Risk-takers and those who thrive on change may feel energized by the uncertainties of starting a business. These individuals tend to view setbacks as opportunities for growth. Conversely, individuals who prefer stability and routine may experience more anxiety in a startup environment.

They may feel more comfortable buying an existing business or franchise, where the risks and unknowns are reduced. Understanding your personality type can help you identify which path aligns better with your emotional strengths.

External circumstances also heavily influence emotional considerations. For example, personal financial stability can affect how much stress you experience. Someone with a solid financial safety net may feel more comfortable taking on the risks of starting a business, while those with limited financial resources may feel overwhelmed by the potential for failure.

Family responsibilities are another significant factor. If you have dependents or other obligations, the uncertainty of entrepreneurship can cause added emotional strain, as your decisions affect not only your own future but also the well-being of others.

Life stage is another important consideration. Younger individuals may be more willing to take on significant risks, knowing they have more time to recover from failures. In contrast, older entrepreneurs may look for a more stable business model with predictable returns.

Emotional resilience also plays a role—those who have faced adversity before may feel more equipped to manage the emotional ups and downs of entrepreneurship, while others may struggle with self-doubt or fear of failure.

Recognizing and managing emotional considerations is key when choosing how to enter the business world. The right decision isn't just about numbers; it's about finding a path that suits your emotional strengths and circumstances.

Chapter Recap

In this chapter, we explored various business entry methods and the factors that influence the decision-making process.

We started by looking at the pros and cons of starting a business. While creating something from scratch offers creative freedom and full control, it also comes with high risks, financial uncertainty, and a steep learning curve.

Buying an existing business, by contrast, provides immediate cash flow and a pre-established market presence but may come with hidden problems and a higher initial cost.

Franchising presents a middle ground, offering brand recognition and operational support, but it also limits personal autonomy due to strict franchisor guidelines. We also discussed the synergies of starting a business and later expanding through acquisitions. This strategy combines the flexibility of a startup with the stability of buying established businesses, allowing for faster growth.

Partnerships and intrapreneurship offer alternative pathways for entrepreneurs. Partnerships allow shared risk and resources, while intrapreneurship lets individuals innovate within an existing company, balancing entrepreneurial freedom with corporate security.

Emotional considerations, such as stress, personality type, and external circumstances like financial stability and family responsibilities, also play a significant role in determining the best entry method for everyone.

Finally, we examined the importance of risk tolerance, which influences your choice between starting or buying a business. Throughout this chapter, we highlighted how entry costs, risk, and emotional factors intersect, shaping the decisions that entrepreneurs must make when entering the business world.

Action Plan

To move forward with your business entry decision, follow these steps:

Assess Your Risk Tolerance: Reflect on your ability to manage potential setbacks. Evaluate your finances to decide how much risk you can tolerate. Consider your personal and professional goals – determining the importance of these goals compared to other life goals can help clarify your risk tolerance.

Evaluate Emotional Considerations: Consider how your personality and external circumstances, such as financial stability and family obligations, affect your ability to take on a new business venture. Decide whether you thrive on uncertainty or prefer more stability.

Analyze Entry Costs: Assess your available capital and how long you can sustain the business before it becomes profitable. Include your ability to raise external funds.

Identify Your Preferred Path: Based on your risk tolerance, emotional readiness, and financial resources, decide whether starting or buying a business is the best option for you. Also consider the franchise option.

Create a Preliminary Framework: Based on your current understanding, develop a basic framework for your decision. Remember, this is not a final decision but rather a set of guiding parameters to refine as you gather more detailed information in the coming chapters. Stay flexible and be ready to adjust your plan as you dive deeper into the specifics of starting or buying a business.

Chapter 2
Starting a Business

"Chase the vision, not the money, the money will end up following you" – Tony Hsieh

Overview

Starting a new business requires careful planning and thoughtful execution. This chapter will guide you through the essential steps to take when embarking on this journey, from idea generation to profitability and growth. Each phase is crucial in laying a solid foundation for your venture and ensuring its long-term success.

The first step, idea generation, involves identifying a market need and developing a business concept that addresses it. This requires not only creativity but also validation to ensure that the idea has potential in the real world. Once an idea is in place, creating a business plan becomes the next critical task. A well-structured business plan serves as a roadmap for your business, outlining goals, strategies, and financial projections.

Legal and regulatory requirements are equally important, as they ensure that your business operates within the boundaries of the law. This section will cover business structure choices, permits, licenses, and compliance with local, state, and federal regulations.

After meeting these requirements, initial funding becomes the focus. Whether you seek loans, investors, or bootstrap your business, securing adequate capital is essential to getting started.

Once funding is in place, it's time to set up operations. This includes everything from finding a location (if necessary) to sourcing suppliers, building a team, and implementing the technology and processes your business needs to run smoothly. As your operations take shape, the focus shifts to achieving breakeven and eventually becoming profitable. This involves managing expenses and maximizing revenue.

Finally, once the business stabilizes, attention will turn to growth. This section will discuss strategies for scaling your business and exploring new opportunities, ensuring that your venture continues to thrive.

This chapter provides a comprehensive guide to each of these stages, equipping you with the knowledge and tools needed to navigate the complexities of starting a business.

Idea Generation and Validation

Generating a business idea is often the first and most critical step in starting a new venture. Many entrepreneurs struggle at this stage, but there are practical techniques that can help make the process smoother and more effective. The key is to combine creativity with research, ensuring that your idea is both innovative and grounded in market reality.

One proven method for idea generation is to identify a problem or gap in the market. Look at your everyday life and consider the pain points people experience. Is there something that often frustrates you or others? Businesses that solve problems tend to be successful because they address a real need. This technique, often referred to as "problem identification," allows you to develop ideas that are both practical and in demand.

Another approach is trend analysis. By staying up to date with market trends and technological advancements, you can find emerging opportunities. For instance, shifts in consumer behavior, economic conditions, or innovative technology can create gaps in the market that a new business could fill. Pay attention to industry reports, news articles, and social media trends to spot these shifts early.

A third method is mind mapping, a more creative approach where you brainstorm various ideas and explore how they might connect. This process helps free up creative thinking and can lead to unexpected combinations of ideas.

For example, you might start with a general concept, like "sustainability," and then branch out to explore related ideas like eco-friendly products, energy-saving technologies, or recycling services. Mind mapping allows you to visually explore multiple avenues without feeling constrained by logical steps.

For those who already have a firm preference or a strong passion, the process of idea generation can be more focused. If you already know what industry or sector excites you, your task is to refine that idea and confirm it. This is where narrowing your focus becomes important. Instead of exploring a wide range of unrelated ideas, concentrate on the one that best aligns with your interests, skills, and long-term goals.

Eliminate unnecessary work by conducting market research early on. Understand the size of the market, the competition, and potential challenges. If your idea still seems promising after this research, move forward with developing it further.

Ultimately, idea generation is not just about finding the perfect concept. It's about aligning your passion and preferences with market demand. By using techniques like problem identification, trend analysis, and mind mapping, you can unlock ideas that fit your strengths. If you already have a clear direction, focusing on validating that idea will save time and prevent unnecessary work.

Basic Feasibility Test

The journey from identifying a business idea to creating a robust business plan begins with a basic feasibility test. This test serves as a bridge between the first spark of an idea and the structured planning phase. It helps determine whether your idea has the potential to become a successful business.

Feasibility refers to whether a business idea can be executed given the available resources, while viability focuses on whether the business can sustain itself and generate profits over time. While both are critical, feasibility is the first step.

The method we will discuss relies on four key pillars that help assess early feasibility. These pillars are often used by financiers—especially those who work closely with entrepreneurs—to filter out applications that are not likely to succeed. This helps avoid wasting time and resources processing business plans that do not meet basic standards.

The four pillars in this basic feasibility test are Product, Market, Entrepreneur's ability to sell, and Entrepreneur's ability to manage. Two of these pillars focus on the business and two focus on the individual behind the idea. By evaluating these factors, entrepreneurs can objectively assess whether they are ready to move forward.

Basic feasibility

	Product	Market
Business	Product	Market
Entrepreneur	Marketing & Sales	Management

Product

The first pillar is the product. For a business to be feasible, there must be a clearly identifiable product or service. Even if the product is still in its conceptual phase, most of its attributes should be defined, such as pricing, packaging, and branding. The product should have a clear value proposition and a target market. At this stage, it is not necessary to have all the details worked out, but the idea should be concrete enough to attract attention and solve a specific problem.

Market

The second pillar is the market. Even without the in-depth research that will come during the business plan phase, the target market should be clear. It's not enough to simply state that there is a "huge market" for the product. The entrepreneur must present some basic facts about the market, such as its size, demographics, and geographic reach. For example, if the product is a specialized fitness app, the entrepreneur should identify how many people are in the target age range, their spending habits, and where they are located. This helps establish whether there is a real demand for the product.

Entrepreneur's Ability to Sell

The third pillar focuses on the entrepreneur's ability to sell. Many entrepreneurs excel at creating products but struggle with selling them. Entrepreneurs with marketing and sales experience have a definite advantage. This pillar assesses whether the entrepreneur can develop a solid marketing strategy and lead a team to execute it.

Entrepreneur's Ability to Manage

The fourth pillar is the entrepreneur's ability to manage. Once the product starts selling, can the entrepreneur manage the business effectively? This includes everything from managing finances and cash flow to handling staff and day-to-day operations.

Running a business requires discipline, organization, and the ability to lead. Even the most promising product will fail if the entrepreneur lacks the skills to manage growth and profitability.

Some financiers argue that all four pillars must be solid for a business idea to pass the feasibility test. Others suggest that at least three pillars should be strong, and the fourth can be developed through mentorship or other support. For example, if an entrepreneur lacks management experience, they might be able to compensate for this by hiring a skilled manager or receiving guidance from a mentor.

The purpose of this chapter is to help readers conduct their own basic feasibility test. This self-assessment is a crucial step before moving on to a full business plan. The key is to stay objective and avoid emotional attachment to an idea that may not be feasible. By analyzing the product, market, and personal abilities, entrepreneurs can save time and resources and position themselves for success.

Creating a Business Plan

A business plan is a structured document that outlines your business goals, strategies, and the steps you'll take to achieve them. It serves as a roadmap for both the entrepreneur and potential investors or partners, showing that you have carefully considered the various aspects of your business.

This document includes everything from your business description and market analysis to financial projections and operational plans. The purpose of a business plan is not only to guide your efforts but also to show others—especially financiers—that your business is viable and well thought out.

Business plans are essential because they offer a detailed view of your venture's potential. Investors, partners, and even lenders will likely require a well-prepared business plan before committing any resources. It also forces the entrepreneur to think through each stage of the business carefully, ensuring that they have a realistic understanding of what is needed for success. Without a solid plan, it is easy to overlook critical elements like market demand, competition, or financial sustainability.

Despite its importance, many entrepreneurs hesitate when it comes to creating a business plan, particularly when they reach the section on financial projections. These projections require forecasting revenue, expenses, and profits—tasks that can feel overwhelming, especially for those without a finance background. Some entrepreneurs may worry that they cannot predict future finances accurately or that their assumptions will be scrutinized. However, even rough estimates are better than none, and they offer a starting point for evaluating the financial feasibility of the business.

To help with this process, a detailed business plan framework is available in Appendix B of this book. This resource will walk you through each section of the business plan, providing guidance and prompting you with the right questions to fill in the details of your own venture.

Additionally, the diagram that follows offers a helpful overview of the business plan framework. Although the full document may seem overwhelming, the diagram provides a clear snapshot of how the five main sections fit together. By breaking down the framework visually, you can better understand how the pieces connect, making it easier to approach each section with confidence.

BUSINESS PLAN FRAMEWORK

1 BUSINESS DESCRIPTION
- Background
- Core activities
- Location
- Product / Service description
- Ownership structure
- Legal considerations

2 OPPORTUNITY
- Client description
- Geographical area
- Total client potential
- Competition
- Competitive advantage
- SWOT analysis

3 MARKETING
- Costing & Pricing
- Sales projections
- Marketing plan

4 MANAGEMENT
- The entrepreneur(s)
- Key operational functions
- Personnel

5 FINANCE
- Financial projections
- Finance required

Let's briefly review the five main sections of the business plan.

Business Description

The business description is the foundation of your plan. Here, you will provide background on your company, including its mission, history, and core activities. You'll also explain the goals you aim to achieve and why you believe this business opportunity is worth pursuing. A clear and concise business description sets the stage for the rest of the plan, helping readers understand the purpose behind your venture and what you aim to accomplish.

Opportunity

The opportunity section outlines the market potential for your product or service. This is where you explain the demand for what you're offering, who your target customers are, and how large the market is. This section gives readers a sense of the business's potential by discussing factors such as demographics, geographic reach, and competition. You should also touch on what makes your business unique—its competitive advantage in the marketplace.

Marketing

A well-thought-out marketing strategy is crucial for the success of any business. In this section, you will describe how you plan to reach your target audience and what methods you'll use to promote your product or service. This includes everything from branding and advertising to social media and event marketing. Your marketing strategy should explain how you will generate sales and build brand awareness, ultimately driving your business toward profitability.

Management

The management section focuses on the people behind the business. Investors and partners want to know whether you, as the entrepreneur, have the skills and experience necessary to execute the plan. This section should highlight your background, along with key members of your team, emphasizing how their skills will contribute to the business's success. Clear roles and responsibilities will show that your business is organized and capable of growth.

Finance

The finance section is often the most daunting part of a business plan. Here, you will lay out your financial projections, detailing how much money is needed to start and run the business and when you expect it to become profitable.

You'll need to include projected cash flow statements, income statements, and balance sheets for at least the first three years. While this section can be challenging, it's crucial to demonstrate that you have a clear financial strategy.

Writing a business plan may seem like a daunting task, but it's an invaluable step in setting up your business for success. By breaking it down into manageable parts, and using the resources provided in this book, you can develop a strong, compelling plan. Remember, every great business starts with a solid foundation, and your business plan is that foundation.

Legal and Regulatory Requirements

When starting a new business, one of the hurdles entrepreneurs face is navigating legal and regulatory requirements. These obligations ensure that your business complies with all local, state, and federal laws.

It's important to differentiate between legal requirements, which include formal laws that must be followed, and regulatory requirements, which are specific rules and standards set by governmental agencies to regulate particular industries.

In the United States, legal requirements typically begin with establishing your business structure. You will need to decide whether your business will be a sole proprietorship, partnership, limited liability company (LLC), or corporation. For LLCs and corporations, you must file Articles of Incorporation or Articles of Organization with your state's Secretary of State office. Once this is completed, you will need to apply for an Employer Identification Number (EIN) from the IRS, which serves as a tax identification number. Each state also has its own requirements regarding business name registration, ensuring that the name is unique and does not conflict with existing trademarks.

In Canada, businesses may need to register either federally or provincially, depending on their scope. Provincial registration is common for smaller, region-based businesses, while federal registration allows for operation across Canada. In the UK, businesses must register with Companies House and apply for a Unique Taxpayer Reference (UTR) from HMRC for tax purposes.

Regulatory requirements vary by industry and location. In the US, these often involve obtaining specific licenses and permits. For example, a restaurant will require health and safety inspections from the local health department, while businesses in the construction industry may need to obtain building permits. Businesses in heavily regulated sectors like finance or pharmaceuticals will require additional approvals, such as licenses from the Financial Industry Regulatory Authority (FINRA) or the Food and Drug Administration (FDA). Additionally, many industries must comply with environmental regulations, and permits may be needed if your business has an impact on the environment.

In both the UK and Canada, regulatory requirements are similar but may involve different governing bodies. In the UK, food businesses must adhere to Food Standards Agency (FSA) guidelines, and environmental permits may be needed for manufacturing. In Canada, food safety is governed by the Canadian Food Inspection Agency (CFIA), while environmental regulations fall under Environment and Climate Change Canada.

Employment laws also form a significant part of regulatory compliance. In the US, you'll need to comply with federal and state labor laws, including minimum wage, overtime pay, and occupational health and safety regulations governed by the Department of Labor (DOL) and Occupational Safety and Health Administration (OSHA). In the UK, these are overseen by the Health and Safety Executive (HSE), while Canada's labor laws vary by province.

Privacy laws, such as the California Consumer Privacy Act (CCPA) in the US, the General Data Protection Regulation (GDPR) in the UK, and PIPEDA in Canada, regulate how businesses manage personal information. If your business collects or processes personal data, you must ensure compliance to avoid hefty fines.

Other legal concerns include drawing up contracts and agreements, such as lease agreements for business premises, employment contracts, and supplier agreements. You'll also need to protect your intellectual property by applying for trademarks, patents, or copyrights. In the US, this is done through the US Patent and Trademark Office (USPTO). Canada and the UK have similar offices: the Canadian Intellectual Property Office and the UK Intellectual Property Office, respectively.

Insurance is another legal requirement in many cases. In the US, businesses must typically have general liability insurance and workers' compensation insurance, especially if they have employees. In the UK, businesses must have employers' liability insurance to cover employee claims, while in Canada, insurance requirements vary by province but generally include workers' compensation and business liability insurance.

Navigating these legal and regulatory requirements can be overwhelming, but ensuring compliance from the start will save time and prevent potential legal issues. Always consult with legal professionals to ensure that your business meets all necessary obligations.

Initial Funding and Financial Planning

Financial planning is at the heart of any successful business, and it's an integral part of the business plan. In the earlier sections, we discussed the importance of preparing detailed financial projections. These projections serve as the foundation for making informed decisions about funding and financial management. In this section, we will build on that foundation to explore how to identify funding needs, source capital, and manage finances effectively.

Funding needs

The first step is to identify funding needs. The capital you need is essentially a combination of start-up costs and working capital. Start-up costs include everything necessary to get the business up and running—this could be plant and equipment, vehicles, initial inventory, permits, licenses, or marketing expenses. Working capital, on the other hand, is the cash needed to cover day-to-day operations until the business reaches breakeven. It includes ongoing expenses such as rent, salaries, utilities, and supplies.

Calculating working capital up to breakeven is essential because you need to ensure that the business can run smoothly until it starts generating enough revenue to cover expenses. If working capital is underestimated, the business may struggle to stay afloat in the critical early months.

Types of funding

Once you have a clear understanding of your funding needs, the next step is to consider the various sources of funding available. Many entrepreneurs start with personal savings or engage in bootstrapping, where they use personal resources to fund the business and grow it organically. Another common choice is seeking funds from family, friends, and angel investors. These individuals may be willing to invest based on trust and a personal relationship, often providing flexible terms.

If you need more substantial funding, bank loans and lines of credit are traditional sources of capital. Banks typically require strong financial projections, collateral, and a good credit history.

For businesses with high growth potential, venture capital and equity financing may be attractive options. These investors provide funding in exchange for a stake in the company, hoping to earn a significant return if the business succeeds.

Additionally, government grants and subsidies may be available, especially if your business operates in sectors like technology, green energy, or innovation. Lastly, crowdfunding platforms such as Kickstarter or GoFundMe allow you to raise small amounts from many people, often in exchange for early product access or other perks.

It is also important to understand the distinction between debt and equity financing. Debt financing involves borrowing money, which must be repaid with interest. The advantage of debt is that you retain full ownership of the business. However, taking on too much debt can strain cash flow and increase financial risk, especially if the business doesn't generate sufficient income early on.

Equity financing, on the other hand, involves selling a portion of ownership in exchange for capital. The key benefit here is that you don't have to repay the funds, but you are giving up a share of future profits and decision-making power. Additionally, equity investors often expect high returns, putting pressure on the business to grow quickly. Choosing between debt and equity depends on your risk tolerance, business model, and long-term vision.

A critical aspect of financial planning is preparing for contingencies. These are funds set aside to cover unexpected expenses or shortfalls in revenue. The general rule of thumb is to set aside at least 10% to 20% of your initial capital as a contingency reserve. This buffer ensures that the business can handle unforeseen challenges such as delayed payments, equipment breakdowns, or economic downturns. Contingency funds provide peace of mind and prevent small hiccups from derailing the entire operation.

Financiers and Investors

When applying for funding, you will need to present certain documentation. Lenders and investors typically expect to see a comprehensive business plan, detailed financial projections, personal financial statements, and information on collateral (if applying for debt). It's also important to be prepared for interviews or initial meetings with financiers. Be ready to explain your business model, demonstrate an understanding of the market, and discuss how their investment or loan will be used. Confidence and preparedness during these interactions can significantly increase your chances of securing the necessary funding.

When meeting with financiers or investors, it's critical that you know your business plan inside and out. As someone who has interviewed hundreds of potential borrowers, I can tell you that nothing raises red flags faster than an entrepreneur who is unfamiliar with the details of their own plan.

It's one thing to hire a professional to help craft the business plan, but if you haven't taken the time to study and understand every aspect of it, from financial projections to market analysis, it shows a lack of commitment. Investors will assume that you're not serious about your business if you can't confidently discuss or defend the details. Being unable to answer questions or clarify small but important points signals that someone else did the heavy lifting for you, and that's inexcusable. If you expect anyone to invest in your vision, you must prove that you are fully engaged and capable of leading the business.

Financial management

The final, and most critical, element of financial planning is ongoing review and monitoring. Even the most well-prepared plans are useless if they aren't reviewed and updated regularly. This is the single biggest weakness of many new businesses: poor financial record-keeping and failure to review performance against projections.

To avoid this pitfall, your business must have systems in place to track actual performance, compare it with forecasts, and produce accurate management accounts. These systems should be implemented from the outset and management accounts must be reviewed monthly to ensure that any issues can be addressed quickly. Staying on top of financial data allows for better decision-making and increases your chances of long-term success.

In conclusion, securing initial funding and managing finances is not just about getting through the initial stages of the business. It's about laying a solid foundation for long-term sustainability and growth. By understanding your funding needs, exploring all available options, and maintaining a disciplined approach to financial management, you can give your business the best chance to succeed.

Setting Up Operations and Launching

The purpose of this book is to help prospective entrepreneurs evaluate their business entry options. In earlier sections, we discussed various aspects of finance, legal requirements, and creating a business plan. Now, we shift focus to a broad view of what it takes to set up operations and launch a business. This section will guide you through some of the key challenges you're likely to face, including infrastructure, technology, building a team, and executing your marketing plan.

One of the first challenges in setting up operations is securing the right infrastructure. Whether you need a physical location, office space, or manufacturing facilities, getting the right infrastructure in place is often more difficult and costly than expected. Location matters: choosing a space that is easily accessible to customers, employees, or suppliers can make or break your business. Beyond the physical space, you'll need to think about utilities, permits, and insurance. Delays with contractors or securing permits can significantly slow down your timeline, so it's crucial to plan carefully and leave room for the unexpected.

Next is the challenge of implementing the necessary technology. Today, nearly every business requires a degree of technological integration, whether it's basic IT systems, point-of-sale (POS) systems, or more complex manufacturing or customer management software. Choosing the right technology can be overwhelming, especially when faced with a wide range of options. It's important to strike a balance between affordability and scalability. You want systems that will meet your needs now but can also grow with your business. Installing and troubleshooting technology often takes more time than planned, so make sure you leave room in your schedule to get everything up and running smoothly.

Building a team is another major hurdle. In earlier sections, we discussed the legal and regulatory requirements for hiring, but the practical challenge is finding the right people. You'll need a mix of skills, from technical expertise to customer service, and hiring employees who fit the company culture is equally important. Recruiting, training, and onboarding can be time-consuming, and many entrepreneurs underestimate the time and effort needed to build a formidable team. A poorly managed hiring process can lead to high turnover, which is costly both financially and in terms of time.

We've already touched on marketing in the business plan but putting that plan into action presents its own set of challenges. You need to translate your marketing strategy into real-world initiatives. This could mean creating and managing social media accounts, organizing promotional events, or developing your website. Execution often takes more resources than expected. For instance, digital marketing campaigns may need more funding, and events might require last-minute adjustments. It's important to be flexible and ready to pivot when certain approaches don't yield the expected results.

As a rule of thumb, entrepreneurs should heed the "rule of three." Whatever your business plan estimates for budget and time, expect reality to exceed those figures. Triple your budget and double your timeframe—this will give you a more realistic understanding of what it will take to launch your business successfully. While this isn't a hard-and-fast rule, ignoring it can lead to costly surprises. The process of setting up operations is full of unexpected obstacles, and being over-prepared is better than finding yourself underfunded or behind schedule.

By taking these challenges into account and approaching each phase with flexibility and foresight, you can avoid some of the common pitfalls that many new businesses face during the setup and launch phases.

Achieving Breakeven and Becoming Profitable

Once your operations are set up and your business is actively generating sales or producing goods, the next major milestone lies ahead: reaching breakeven.

This is one of the most significant moments in the life of any business because it marks the point at which your company stops losing money and starts to operate at a profit. After setting up operations, achieving breakeven becomes the most critical goal you should work toward, as it is the tipping point between financial strain and sustainability.

So, what exactly is breakeven? In simple terms, it's the level of sales or revenue your business needs to generate to cover all its costs. Up until that point, your business is spending more than it earns, often referred to as "burning money." This burn period is expected and can last for several months or even years, depending on the business model. Once you reach breakeven, the revenue starts to exceed the costs, and from there, the business can finally turn a profit. In other words, prior to breakeven, your business is in negative cash flow, and after breakeven, it moves into positive cash flow.

A key factor in managing your path to breakeven is understanding your business's burn rate. The burn rate is the rate at which a company is spending its available capital. Different businesses have different burn rates based on their operational needs.

For example, a software startup may have a lower burn rate due to its minimal physical infrastructure, but it might still face significant costs in areas like development, testing, and slow customer acquisition. On the other end of the spectrum, a manufacturing business might have a higher burn rate not only because of expensive machinery and inventory but also due to high operating costs, long production cycles, and potentially slow growth in sales.

Additionally, some industries require extensive testing and certification, which can delay revenue generation. Understanding your burn rate helps you predict how long you can sustain operations before running out of funds and how quickly you need to reach breakeven.

Reaching breakeven earlier than expected can be a game-changer for a business. It reduces the amount of capital you need to sustain operations, giving you more room to invest in growth or safeguard against unforeseen challenges. It also signals that your business model is functioning as planned or even exceeding expectations.

On the flip side, reaching breakeven later than planned can strain your resources, requiring you to seek additional funding or cut costs to stay afloat. Delays in reaching breakeven may also force you to reconsider certain aspects of your strategy, such as pricing, marketing, or operational efficiency.

However, it's important to recognize that breakeven should be closely monitored. Sometimes, a business may temporarily reach breakeven due to a seasonal bump in sales or a short-term contract. While this can provide a momentary boost, it doesn't necessarily indicate sustained growth. Seasonal businesses, such as retail or tourism companies, might hit breakeven during their peak season, only to drop back into negative cash flow during the off-season. It's essential to track performance consistently to ensure that breakeven is achieved and maintained through sustained growth rather than temporary spikes in revenue.

In conclusion, achieving breakeven is the critical moment when your business transitions from burning capital to generating profit. It is a key indicator of your business's financial health and sustainability. By understanding your burn rate and closely checking your progress toward breakeven, you can make informed decisions that help you stay on track and guide your business to profitability.

Growth and Long-Term Profitability

Once breakeven is reached and sustained over a period, the entrepreneur's focus can shift toward growth and profitability. Reaching this stage is a significant milestone, but it's only the beginning of the next phase of business development.

Becoming profitable is undoubtedly a momentous occasion for any business. It signifies that the company is no longer burning through capital and is now generating enough revenue to cover its costs. But the excitement of profitability can fade quickly if it's not stable and sustainable. Temporary profitability—perhaps due to a one-time contract or seasonal sales—is not the same as long-term financial health. Therefore, the focus should shift to ensuring that the business stays profitable over time, even as market conditions change.

Ensuring long-term stability requires strong and effective management. The first key area to focus on is operational efficiency. As the business grows, operational complexities increase. You need systems in place that can handle a larger volume of sales, customers, or product production without creating bottlenecks. This could involve streamlining processes, improving supply chain management, or investing in modern technology. Continuous process improvement is essential to keep costs under control and maintain profitability.

Another critical aspect is financial management. Monitoring cash flow, profits, and expenses must remain a priority. Regular reviews of financial statements and forecasts will help ensure that the business remains on track. Proper expense management is vital as businesses often experience higher costs during periods of rapid growth. It's easy to overspend in the rush to expand, so discipline in budgeting and spending is crucial. Additionally, keeping an eye on working capital will ensure that the business doesn't run into liquidity issues as it grows.

Leadership and team management also play a vital role in sustaining profitability. As the business expands, the founder may no longer be able to manage every aspect of operations. This is where building a capable leadership team becomes essential. Delegating responsibility to experienced managers allows the founder to focus on strategy and long-term planning rather than day-to-day tasks. It also helps ensure that various parts of the business—such as marketing, finance, and operations—are running smoothly and aligned with the company's growth objectives.

In addition, market adaptation is essential for long-term stability. Markets evolve, and customer needs change over time. To stay profitable, a business must remain agile and adaptable. This could involve introducing new products or services, exploring new markets, or staying ahead of competitors with innovative strategies. Consistently gathering and analyzing market data will help the business make informed decisions and stay relevant in its industry.

Lastly, keeping an eye on customer satisfaction is crucial. Growth often brings new customers and keeping them satisfied is key to generating repeat business and long-term revenue. Implementing customer feedback loops and maintaining strong relationships with your client base will help ensure sustained growth and stability.

In summary, achieving profitability is a significant milestone, but maintaining that profitability over the long term requires careful management. Operational efficiency, strong financial discipline, capable leadership, adaptability to market changes, and customer satisfaction are all essential elements for ensuring that your business stays profitable and sustainable in the long run.

Chapter Recap

In this chapter, we've covered the key aspects of starting a new business, guiding prospective entrepreneurs from the initial idea to growth and profitability.

The journey begins with idea generation, where you find a market need and develop a concept that addresses it. We discussed various techniques for idea validation, such as problem identification, trend analysis, and mind mapping, ensuring that your idea has both creativity and real-world potential.

Next, we moved on to conducting a basic feasibility test, which helps determine whether your business idea is executable. The test focuses on four pillars: product, market, the entrepreneur's ability to sell, and the entrepreneur's ability to manage. This self-assessment is crucial before committing to a full business plan, helping to save time and resources by filtering out ideas that may not be feasible.

We also explored the importance of creating a comprehensive business plan, which serves as a roadmap for both you and potential investors. It includes key sections like business description, market opportunity, marketing, management, and finance. While the process can seem daunting, especially when it comes to financial projections, it's essential for setting a solid foundation for your business.

The chapter then touched on legal and regulatory requirements, highlighting the steps you need to take to ensure your business complies with local, state, and federal laws. From choosing a business structure to obtaining necessary permits and licenses, this section provided a broad overview of how to stay compliant.

Finally, we covered initial funding and financial planning, focusing on identifying funding needs and exploring various sources of capital. We also emphasized the importance of contingency funds and keeping a disciplined approach to financial management as you achieve breakeven and prepare for growth.

Action plan

Review the preliminary framework you completed after Chapter 1 and adjust it as required.

Chapter 3
Buying a Business

"It's far better to buy a wonderful company at a fair price than a fair company at a wonderful price" – Warren Buffett

Overview

In the journey of evaluating business entry options, buying a business can present many advantages compared to starting one from scratch. Chapter 3 focuses on this avenue of business ownership and explores the complexities involved in purchasing an established venture. By the end of this chapter, you will have a clear understanding of the various aspects you must consider before making such an investment.

We begin by discussing how to find and evaluate businesses for sale. Identifying the right business is more than just finding something available. You must align the business opportunity with your skills, experience, and personal goals. We will guide you on what to look for and how to approach the search strategically.

Next, we delve into valuing a business. This is a critical step because overpaying for a business can severely affect your future profitability. We will discuss key valuation methods and how to assess if a business is priced fairly.

Once a basic agreement is reached with the seller, the due diligence process begins. Thorough due diligence ensures that you know exactly what you are buying. From financial records to operational issues, this section will walk you through the vital areas you should investigate. A detailed checklist is available in Appendix B: Resources.

Legal considerations are also essential. From structuring the purchase agreement to understanding liabilities, we will cover what you need to ensure a legally sound transaction.

Afterward, negotiating the purchase price comes into play. You will learn effective strategies to negotiate a fair price, ensuring you get value for your money.

Finally, we will explore how to finance the acquisition and transition operations.

Finding and Evaluating Businesses for Sale

When considering buying a business, the first challenge is often finding a suitable one for sale. The search process involves multiple approaches, from online platforms to personal networks. It's important to use a variety of methods to increase your chances of finding the right fit.

Online marketplaces dedicated to business sales are excellent resources. Websites such as BizBuySell and BizQuest (primarily in the US), BusinessesForSale (global, but especially strong in the UK and Canada), and LoopNet are good places to start. These platforms list thousands of businesses for sale, often with detailed descriptions, financial information, and contact details.

Use Google to search for industry-specific platforms. For a broader reach, some regional classified ads or business sections of newspapers may also include listings.

Next, consider subscribing to industry newsletters or joining associations related to your field of interest. Industry-specific associations sometimes circulate information on businesses for sale, especially those within niche markets. You could also attend business expos or conventions, which offer a terrific opportunity to network with sellers or brokers.

Networking within your professional circles or even with your competitors can also reveal opportunities. Sometimes, businesses are sold privately, and these deals might never reach public listings. A simple conversation with someone in the industry could open doors to finding a business for sale.

Another helpful method is engaging with business brokers. A good business broker does more than list businesses; they understand the intricacies of the market and often have access to listings not found elsewhere. Brokers in the US, Canada, and the UK typically offer services tailored to their regions. Still, the principle remains the same—they streamline the process and help connect buyers with sellers. Furthermore, brokers often have a comprehensive understanding of the business they are selling, giving you a head start in your evaluation process.

Before any detailed information is shared or meetings with the seller are arranged, brokers or sellers will likely require a letter of intent (LOI). This document serves as an initial agreement outlining your interest in buying the business. It typically includes non-disclosure or confidentiality clauses, ensuring that any sensitive information provided remains confidential. The LOI is not legally binding but shows the seller that you are serious about moving forward. Only after signing this document can you usually gain access to the more detailed financial records or be allowed to conduct a site visit.

With an LOI finalized, the next step is to conduct a preliminary evaluation. This step is not as detailed as full due diligence but helps you decide if it's worth pursuing further. First, request a discussion with the seller. In this conversation, ask about the business's key aspects—its history, financial performance, and customer base. Try to get a sense of why the seller is interested in selling. Sometimes, this reveals underlying issues you might want to avoid.

A site inspection should follow. Visiting the business premises allows you to assess operational workflows, the condition of physical assets, and staff morale. These factors might be partially reflected in the information provided but are crucial for determining the business's potential. For example, poor staff morale or rundown equipment may indicate problems that will require immediate investment.

In addition, a basic desktop analysis will be performed. Review the provided financial statements to check for any glaring red flags, such as consistent year-over-year losses. Compare the business's performance with industry standards to gauge its relative position in the market. Business brokers often provide prospective buyers with a helpful overview of the business for sale to facilitate this basic analysis.

At this early stage, you should create a rudimentary plan to fund the transaction. Please share it with the broker, knowledgeable friends, or a mentor to get an idea of whether it is workable.

In summary, finding the right business for sale requires a broad search strategy, while evaluating it involves a combination of conversations, site visits, and financial assessments. Each step brings you closer to making an informed decision about whether the business is a workable purchase.

Due Diligence Investigation (DDI)

Once the preliminary evaluation is completed to your satisfaction, the next crucial step is the Due Diligence Investigation (DDI). This phase is essential in thoroughly verifying every aspect of the business before finalizing any decision.

Purchase Agreement

Before beginning the DDI, the broker and seller will typically require more than just a Letter of Intent (LOI). In most cases, you will need to sign a purchase agreement, and a deposit might even be requested. Now, you might ask, "How can an agreement be signed before verifying all the details?" The answer lies in suspensive conditions.

The most critical part of the purchase agreement is these suspensive conditions. These clauses state that the agreement only takes effect if specific conditions are met. If any of these conditions are not fulfilled, the agreement becomes null, and the deposit is refunded. While this is a basic explanation, consulting legal counsel is always advised to understand the implications of the agreement thoroughly. Once you're satisfied with the purchase agreement, your focus can shift to the DDI.

Importance of the DDI

The DDI is an invaluable tool for buyers. It provides the most comprehensive method for making an informed decision about the purchase. Not only does it help ensure that the purchase agreement is aligned with the risks involved, but it also clarifies those risks. However, it's essential to understand that **a DDI won't eliminate risks. Instead, it will help you quantify and qualify them**.

To illustrate its significance, consider how lenders approach risk. For financial institutions that require collateral exceeding 100% of the loan (typically through immovable property), the DDI might be limited to basic business verification and a short site visit. On the other hand, lenders relying on business viability instead of full collateral coverage will demand a more in-depth DDI that cannot be compromised.

What the DDI Entails

An investment decision usually hinges on a satisfactory due diligence investigation. This involves verifying and analyzing the representations, statements, figures, documents, reports, opinions, intentions, and even the physical environment of the business. The goal is for the buyer or financier to make a prudent and informed decision.

For simpler or smaller transactions, an experienced buyer may conduct the DDI without the need for external help. However, it's important to recognize how large firms, especially private equity firms, conduct a DDI. They typically assemble a team of experts, including finance, legal, technical, and marketing specialists, to ensure the investigation is thorough.

The checklist in Appendix B: Resources can help you through the DDI process.

A DDI should be methodical and carefully planned. Some information can be gathered and verified before even meeting with the seller. For instance, a bank reference check on the business and credit checks on both the seller and the business can be done in advance, provided that the seller gives written permission.

When it comes to these checks, the approach varies slightly across regions:

In the United States, credit checks are commonly done through credit reporting agencies, focusing on both the business and personal credit history of the seller. Bank references, with seller consent, are requested directly from banks.

In Canada, the process is much the same, with a heavy focus on the business's financial obligations. Privacy laws necessitate explicit permission from the seller for both credit and bank checks.

In the UK, bank reference checks are more restricted due to strict privacy regulations, but credit checks remain just as available and have similar permission requirements.

Navigating Seller Resistance

It's common for sellers to want to rush the DDI process. This could be due to their lack of understanding about its importance or because they are eager to close the deal. Some may even take the investigation personally, feeling that it implies distrust. In cases where the seller or broker has provided less-than-complete information initially, they may try to downplay or hide specific facts during the DDI.

Certain sellers may also have an inflated sense of their entrepreneurial abilities, especially in marketing. They might expect the buyer to take their word at face value without questioning or verifying figures. However, as a buyer, you must remain firm. Every piece of information needs to be thoroughly vetted, and there's no room for assumptions.

Allow sufficient time to complete an inclusive DDI. Some pieces of information may take days or even weeks to gather, so don't let the seller pressure you into rushing.

Final Steps: Documenting and Filing

Once your DDI is complete, ensure all working papers are well-organized and properly filed. This final step in the DDI process is a matter of good administration. Keeping a thorough record of the investigation will provide valuable reference material in the future, particularly if any issues arise after the deal is finalized.

In summary, a Due Diligence Investigation is a vital part of any business acquisition process. It allows you to understand the risks, verify critical details, and make a well-informed decision.

Though it can be time-consuming and sometimes costly, the effort you put into a thorough DDI is always worth it in the long run. By carefully planning and carrying out the investigation, you can ensure that the business you're buying aligns with your expectations.

Business Valuation

Now that the DDI is completed, you can proceed with valuing the business. This chapter focuses on a practical and straightforward method for small business valuation, offering insight into how new entrepreneurs and small business owners, rather than large corporations or venture capital practitioners, can effectively estimate a business's value.

Unlike big corporations with extensive histories and stable profit records, small businesses require a simplified and accessible valuation approach that is both practical and considerate of their unique circumstances.

For background, it's worth noting the standard methods used for valuing publicly traded companies and large corporations. In these cases, the most common methods include the Discounted Cash Flow (DCF) analysis, where future cash flows are estimated and discounted back to their present value. Another common approach is Comparative Company Analysis, which involves comparing the company to similar businesses in the industry based on financial metrics like earnings and revenue. Additionally, precedent transactions are used, which look at the valuations of comparable companies that have been recently acquired. While these methods are highly detailed and data-intensive, they don't necessarily apply well to small businesses due to the unique characteristics of the latter.

Industry and sector-specific methods can also play a role in business valuation. For instance, restaurants are often valued using a multiple of their annual sales or a price-to-earnings ratio that factors in profitability, location, and customer base. In the tech sector, particularly for Amazon or Kindle Direct Publishing (KDP) accounts, valuation is commonly based on a multiple of recurring revenue. Similarly, SaaS (Software as a Service) companies are frequently valued using monthly or annual recurring revenue (MRR or ARR) as a key indicator, often combined with customer acquisition costs and churn rates.

Other sectors, such as retail, might rely on inventory and foot traffic, while professional service businesses may be valued based on client contracts and the owner's role in the business. These industry-specific approaches provide tailored frameworks for valuation but may vary in applicability depending on the business model and market dynamics.

For small businesses, valuation techniques tend to be more straightforward. Standard methods include the asset-based approach, where the value of the business's assets is added up, and the income-based approach, where the value is determined based on the income the business generates.

Small businesses typically lack the long-term stability and vast profit histories of large corporations, making future projections riskier. As a result, valuing a small business requires a secure and confident focus on historical data and tangible factors, ensuring a reliable valuation process.

The following recommended valuation method simplifies the process and provides a practical tool for small businesses. Appendix B: Resources gives you access to an Excel spreadsheet with this method and a Word document that discusses it.

This method does not rely on extensive financial forecasts but instead uses seven key inputs to estimate the business's value.

The Seven Key Inputs

1. **Net Profit** The net profit is one of the most critical factors in this valuation method. It is the average annual profit that a buyer can reasonably expect to make. For small businesses, this figure is typically quoted before tax, interest, and owner's remuneration. In most cases, historic profits are used unless the business has a well-established track record and a reliable business plan. Using projected profits could overestimate the business's value, which is why buyers are recommended to rely on historical numbers to avoid unrealistic expectations.

2. **Fixed Assets** The value of the fixed assets, such as machinery, property, and equipment, is another part.

These assets must be valued based on their market value, not book value, replacement cost, or forced sale value. Market value is the price the assets would fetch in an open market without any pressure for a quick sale.

3. **Average Inventory** Inventory levels can fluctuate, so it is crucial to figure out the average inventory required for the business to operate normally. If the business is overstocked, the inventory needs to be adjusted to a reasonable level.

4. **Goodwill Factor** Goodwill reflects the intangible value of the business, such as brand reputation, customer loyalty, and intellectual property. This valuation uses a subjective goodwill factor ranging from 1 to 3, where 1 represents 12 months, and 3 means 36 months. The exact factor chosen also depends on characteristics such as industry conditions, product uniqueness, and competition. In some rare cases, a factor higher than 3 may be justified, but this is generally reserved for businesses with significant competitive advantages.

5. **Required Rate of Return** This rate represents the pre-tax rate of return expected by the buyer, typically ranging between 20% and 50%, depending on the business's risk profile and the buyer's risk appetite. Businesses perceived to be riskier will have higher required rates of return, as the buyer will want compensation for the extra risk being taken on.

6. **Risk-Free Rate of Return** The risk-free rate of return is the return a buyer could get from a short-term government bond, which is considered to have no risk of default. This figure is used to measure the opportunity cost—the return the buyer forgoes by investing in the business instead of

a risk-free asset. This provides context for understanding the relative risk of the business investment.

7. **Manager's Salary** The manager's salary represents the cost of hiring a manager to run the business in the owner's absence. This figure is vital because it helps distinguish the owner's earnings from the business's profitability. Note that, for this valuation method, it is a fictitious manager and has nothing to do with the existing personnel or the involvement of the present or new owner.

The Three Valuation Methods

1. **Extra Earnings Potential (EEP)** The extra earnings potential method calculates the business's potential for generating additional income. It finds the value of the business's goodwill by calculating how much extra income the buyer could reasonably expect to earn. Once goodwill is calculated, the value of the business's fixed assets and inventory is added to determine the total value. In this method, the net profit and asset value carry the most weight.

2. **Return on Investment (ROI)** The return on investment method asks the question, "How much should I invest in this business to achieve my desired pre-tax rate of return?" The buyer uses this method to decide if the business can meet their expectations for return. This method focuses heavily on the required rate of return and net profit, providing a clear picture of whether the investment is likely to meet financial goals.

3. **Payback Period** The payback period method calculates how long it will take for the buyer to recoup their

investment in the business. This is particularly useful for small companies where liquidity is a concern. The method heavily emphasizes the goodwill factor and net profit, giving the buyer an idea of how quickly they will recover their initial outlay.

Calculating the Average Value

Once the three valuation methods are completed, the next step is to calculate the arithmetic average of the values. This average tends to give a well-rounded estimate of the business's worth. By averaging the results, the buyer gains a clearer picture of the business's value while accounting for variations in each method's assumptions.

Transaction Structure – Inventory

Although the value of inventory is determined during the valuation process, it is still a variable and must be confirmed through a physical count on the date of the takeover. For this reason, inventory is excluded from the final business value, and the purchase price will typically read "purchase price of $XXX plus inventory." This ensures that the buyer only pays for the inventory they receive on the date of the takeover.

Transaction Structure – Debtors, Creditors, and Cash

Debtors, creditors, and cash are excluded from the valuation for practical reasons. On the takeover date, the buyer will start fresh with new debtors' and creditors' books, while the seller will collect pre-existing debts and pay outstanding creditors. This approach minimizes the risk of bad debts and understated liabilities for the buyer. Cash is also excluded from the transaction since it doesn't make sense for a buyer to pay for cash reserves.

Summary

This valuation method provides a practical tool for small businesses, allowing new entrepreneurs to make informed decisions. While this chapter outlines the fundamental principles, it is essential to remember that business valuation and deal structuring are complex subjects that require further research and learning. The purpose of this book is to introduce new entrepreneurs to the concept of business valuation, particularly when buying a business. Still, there are many more details to explore in specialized resources.

In conclusion, net profit is the most critical factor in all three valuation methods. Sellers may push to use future profits, but buyers should base their calculations on historical data to avoid inflated valuations.

Legal Considerations

The legal considerations discussed here pertain specifically to the process of buying a business rather than the broader legal and regulatory requirements that we covered in Chapter 2. Those requirements will equally apply to the business being bought, whether a legal entity or its assets.

Hopefully, by this stage, your due diligence investigation (DDI) has confirmed that the business meets these legal and regulatory standards and that all necessary licenses, permits, and registrations can be transferred to the new owner—whether an individual or another legal entity.

What to buy

One critical legal decision you will face when buying a business is whether to buy the entire legal entity or just its specified assets.

If you buy the legal entity, you take ownership of the company's shares or membership interests (depending on the structure), which includes everything associated with that business—assets, liabilities, contracts, and even potential hidden issues.

This option comes with significant risks. For instance, buying the legal entity may expose you to past liabilities, such as unresolved legal disputes or outstanding tax obligations, even if they were unknown to you at the time of purchase.

On the other hand, buying only specified assets—typically fixed assets, inventory, and other business essentials—is generally a safer option. This is commonly structured as an Asset Purchase Agreement (APA). With an APA, you select the assets you want to buy, which limits your exposure to liabilities.

By leaving behind unwanted liabilities or obligations, you have more control over what you are taking on. However, the scope of the agreement will define what happens to existing creditors, contracts, and employees.

It's important to differentiate between buying individual assets and acquiring business assets as a going concern. Buying individual assets could mean just buying specified equipment or inventory while buying a business as a going concern includes all assets necessary to continue operations seamlessly. The latter choice generally offers a smoother transition, as the business continues to operate as usual after the transfer of ownership.

Buyer protection

Unknown or undisclosed liabilities are another critical aspect of legal considerations. In the US[1] , Canada[2] , and the UK[3] , buyers are protected against undisclosed liabilities to some extent, depending on the structure of the deal. In asset purchases, liabilities generally remain with the seller unless explicitly transferred to the buyer. This means you can usually avoid taking on the seller's debts, pending lawsuits, or tax liabilities.

Other protections, such as warranties and indemnities in the purchase agreement, are vital in APAs. These legal mechanisms can help shield you from liabilities that may arise after the sale.

An APA is often recommended for small businesses unless there

---

1. **Bulk Sales Laws**: Some states have laws that protect creditors when a business sells most or all its assets outside the ordinary course of business. These laws require the buyer to notify creditors of the sale. **Asset Purchase Agreements (APAs)**: In most asset sales, the agreement will outline the buyer's and seller's obligations. The buyer typically assumes only the liabilities explicitly agreed upon, while the seller remains responsible for their debts. If creditors exist, the seller may have to settle those debts before the sale closes. **Successor Liability**: In certain cases, courts may impose successor liability on a buyer if the transaction is seen as a de facto merger or if the buyer explicitly assumes liabilities.

2. **Asset Purchase Agreements (APAs)**: Like the U.S., buyers in Canada can avoid assuming the seller's debts by structuring the purchase as an asset sale. The buyer and seller agree on which liabilities will be transferred. By default, liabilities stay with the seller unless otherwise negotiated.

3. **TUPE (Transfer of Undertakings - Protection of Employment Regulations)**: When buying a business, especially one that involves transferring employees, the UK's TUPE regulations may apply. These regulations protect employees, ensuring their rights are transferred to the new employer. **Asset Purchase Agreements (APAs)**: Like in the U.S. and Canada, buyers can avoid assuming liabilities by structuring the sale as an asset purchase and carefully specifying in the APA which liabilities are being assumed. The buyer generally does not assume liabilities unless explicitly agreed to.

is a compelling reason to buy the legal entity itself. The ability to buy the business assets and leave behind unwanted obligations makes this a popular choice for small business acquisitions.

However, it's essential to recognize that buying assets rather than an entire entity can have tax implications. For example, in some jurisdictions, asset purchases may lead to higher taxes than equity purchases because of how gains are classified. Tax treatment varies across the US, Canada, and the UK, so understanding the tax implications of your deal structure is crucial and should be researched in advance.

Non-compete and non-solicitation clauses are critical parts of a business purchase agreement. These clauses prevent the seller from starting a competing business or poaching employees or customers after the sale. In the US, these clauses are generally enforceable as long as they are reasonable in scope, time, and geography. In the UK and Canada, the enforceability of non-compete clauses is often more limited, requiring stricter scrutiny to ensure they do not excessively restrict competition. Regardless of jurisdiction, these clauses protect the buyer from unfair competition by the seller, preserving the value of the business post-purchase.

Employees

Another essential aspect to consider is employee rights and obligations. When buying a business, mainly if it's a going concern, you will likely inherit its employees. In the UK and parts of Canada, employment laws favor employee protection, meaning that employee contracts, rights, and obligations transfer with the business. In the US, employment laws vary by state, but federal law does provide certain protections. Buyers should review existing employee contracts and understand their obligations to avoid legal issues. This might include dealing with accrued vacation pay and severance packages and understanding any union agreements, if applicable.

The agreement

Lastly, it is essential to ensure that the terms of the purchase agreement are clear on what is being bought, whether it's assets, inventory, or the entire legal entity. The contract should explicitly outline what is included in the sale and, equally important, what is not included.

It is also critical to thoroughly understand the warranties, representations, and indemnities provided by the seller. These provisions protect you if there are any misrepresentations or unexpected issues after the purchase. Indemnities, for example, offer protection if you discover that certain liabilities weren't disclosed before the sale. Warranties ensure that the seller has provided accurate information about the business's operations, financials, and legal status. Please keep in mind that no warranty or indemnity can replace a thorough DDI.

Engaging experienced legal counsel is non-negotiable at this stage to ensure that all these details are adequately addressed.

Summary

When buying a business, several legal factors must be considered beyond the general regulatory requirements discussed in Chapter 2. From deciding between an asset purchase and buying the legal entity to ensuring you are protected from liabilities, every aspect requires careful attention. Non-compete clauses, employee rights, and clear terms in the purchase agreement are just as critical. Legal counsel will help guide you through these complexities, ensuring a smooth and secure transaction.

Negotiating the Purchase Price

In the typical sequence of events when buying a business, a basic purchase agreement is usually signed early in the process. This agreement, often non-binding, sets the initial terms and grants the buyer the opportunity to conduct a thorough due diligence investigation (DDI).

Once the DDI is complete, the buyer should have a clear understanding of the business's financial health, operational status, and any potential risks or liabilities. Armed with this information, the buyer can perform an accurate valuation of the business and decide on a fair price to offer. This revised price will be reflected in the final purchase agreement.

It is not uncommon for the final price to differ from the original offer. The DDI may reveal information that was either missing or less favorable than initially presented by the seller. For instance, there may be undisclosed liabilities, outdated equipment, or a customer base that is not as strong as initially stated. Issues such as these often lead to a lower offer than the original price, and it is at this stage that negotiations genuinely begin.

Negotiating a lower price requires solid justification. The buyer cannot expect the seller to accept a reduced offer without clear, documented reasons. This means that the buyer must be prepared to present findings from the DDI and explain how these findings affect the valuation. For example, if the DDI uncovered financial discrepancies or operational inefficiencies, the buyer should explain how these issues reduce the business's overall worth. Proper preparation is essential here. Detailed reports and well-organized documentation will strengthen the buyer's position, while verbal arguments alone are unlikely to convince the seller.

At this point, the seller has several options. They can accept the buyer's revised offer, reject it outright, or enter negotiations to find a middle ground.

If the seller rejects the offer, the buyer may need to decide whether to share their valuation method. There are pros and cons to sharing this information. On one hand, explaining the valuation method can provide transparency and build trust, which might encourage the seller to reconsider their stance. On the other hand, revealing too much can expose the buyer's thought process, giving the seller leverage to counter-argue specific points. In many cases, buyers opt to share only a general explanation of their valuation, keeping the finer details private.

Several tactics can be helpful when negotiating the purchase price of a small business. One common approach is to ask for seller financing, where the seller agrees to finance a part of the purchase price over a specified period. This can make the deal more attractive for the buyer while offering the seller a steady income stream post-sale. Another tactic is to request concessions on other terms, such as extended transition support or inventory adjustments, in exchange for a slightly higher price. Flexibility on non-monetary aspects can often lead to a more favorable deal overall.

In summary, negotiating the purchase price is a critical step in buying a business. If the due diligence process reveals new information, the closing price may differ from the initial offer. Buyers must be well-prepared, providing documented reasons for any price adjustments. By using a combination of negotiation tactics, buyers can often find a price that satisfies both parties and closes the deal.

Financing the Acquisition

So, the seller accepted your offer? Congratulations! Now comes the next major step: fulfilling the payment terms of the deal.

If you're like many buyers, you may need to raise finance for part or all of the purchase price. When this is the case, your purchase agreement must include a clause stating that the entire agreement is subject to successfully raising the required finance. This clause protects you from being locked into a deal you can't fund. Typically, a time limit is included, giving you a set period to secure the funds before the deal falls through.

The sources of funds for buying a business are similar to those for starting a new business. You can rely on personal savings, approach friends and family, seek out loans from banks, or even look for equity investors. The key difference is in the risk profile. An established business with a track record of earnings and an existing customer base is seen as less risky than a start-up. This can make it easier to raise finance, as lenders or investors may feel more confident about the business's ability to generate a return. However, your personal risk tolerance and financial situation will influence which funding route you choose.

One way to raise finance is to use the business's own assets as collateral. This is a common method in the US, Canada, and the UK, though the specifics may differ slightly between countries. In the US, for instance, businesses may be able to use equipment, inventory, or real estate as security for a loan. Similar options exist in the UK and Canada, but lenders might apply different valuations to the assets.

This form of asset-backed financing can be attractive because it ties the loan to the business itself rather than your personal finances. However, be aware that lenders might insist on personal guarantees even if business assets are offered as collateral.

Another possibility to consider is owner financing (also known as seller financing). In this scenario, the seller agrees to finance a part of the purchase price, allowing you to pay them over time. This arrangement can range from complete financing—where the seller provides all the funds needed, and you repay them according to a schedule—to partial financing, where the seller covers only a small part of the purchase price. This type of financing is common in small business acquisitions, especially when traditional financing options are limited or the business's financials are not strong enough to secure a bank loan.

A common form of owner financing is a suspensive sale agreement, where ownership of the business is transferred to the buyer only after the total purchase price is paid. This protects the seller's interests but can limit the buyer's control until full payment is made. In the US, this agreement is sometimes referred to as an installment sale. In Canada and the UK, the terms are similar, but local legal frameworks may influence how such contracts are structured. The primary benefit of owner financing is that it reduces the upfront financial burden for the buyer. The downside is that it could negatively affect the business's cash flow if not appropriately structured, over an acceptable period, and at a fair interest rate.

It's also important to consider that financiers may require a business plan, even though you are buying an existing business rather than starting one from scratch. Lenders and investors will want to know how you plan to manage and grow the business after the acquisition. A solid business plan should outline how you'll handle operations, address any issues identified during due diligence, and ensure profitability.

Just as with a start-up, a well-crafted plan reassures financiers that their investment or loan is secure. The significant difference is that with an established business, your plan can draw on existing data and customer relationships, making it more grounded than a start-up projection.

In conclusion, financing the acquisition of a business involves many options. Whether you use personal savings, business loans, or owner financing, the key is to choose the path that aligns with your financial goals and the risk profile of the business. Remember to include a financing contingency in your purchase agreement to protect yourself in case funding falls through. With the right plan in place, you'll be well on your way to finalizing your acquisition and taking ownership of your new business.

Transitioning Operations and Integration

The excitement of becoming the new owner is undeniable now that all the formalities have been finalized. As the new leader, you're stepping into a well-established business with systems, employees, and customers already in place. But now the real work begins—transitioning operations and integrating yourself into the business smoothly.

So, what does "transitioning operations" actually mean? It's the process of ensuring that the business continues to function effectively under your ownership. This involves understanding the business's day-to-day operations, addressing any gaps or inefficiencies, and ensuring there's minimal disruption to customers and employees. Integration is about becoming part of the business—making sure you, as the new owner, are accepted by employees, customers, suppliers, and any other stakeholders.

Several factors can influence how well this transition goes. On the positive side, if the business already has a strong, loyal team in place, the handover will be smoother. Established relationships with suppliers and customers will also help ensure continuity. However, challenges arise if the previous owner is heavily involved in the daily operations. In such cases, employees, suppliers, and customers might be uncertain about the future, creating tension. Resistance to new leadership is another potential issue, particularly if you plan to introduce changes that disrupt long-standing practices.

A vital part of the transition process is the handover. This is often covered in the purchase agreement, and it outlines the role the seller will play during this critical period. Having the seller actively involved in the handover is beneficial. Their knowledge and expertise can be invaluable as you learn the ropes, especially in areas like understanding key clients, managing supplier relationships, and handling the finer details of the business's operations. It's common for a purchase agreement to include a period of seller involvement post-sale, typically ranging from a few months to up to a year. Initially, the seller may be involved full-time, with their role gradually tapering off as you gain confidence and fully integrate into the business.

Effective communication is essential during this time, particularly when it comes to informing all relevant parties—employees, suppliers, clients, and service providers—about the change in ownership. Internally, employees should be the first to know, and it's best to meet with them in person or virtually if needed. Clearly communicate your vision for the business, address any concerns, and outline how the transition will unfold. For external stakeholders like suppliers and customers, timely communication is equally important. Reassure them that the business will continue to operate as usual and that you are committed to maintaining existing relationships.

When it comes to marketing, announcing an ownership change can be tricky. In most cases, advertising that the business is under new ownership is only advisable if there is a clear reason, such as a rebranding effort or major changes in the business model. Customers might perceive an ownership change as a signal of instability, which could negatively impact their loyalty. Instead, it's better to focus on continuity and reliability, ensuring that customers continue to receive the same level of service they've come to expect.

In summary, transitioning operations and integrating yourself as the new owner is a crucial process that sets the tone for the business's future. Success depends on clear communication, learning from the seller, and maintaining solid relationships with employees and stakeholders. A smooth transition will help solidify your position and ensure the continued success of the business.

Chapter Recap

In Chapter 3, we examined the essential aspects of buying an established business, beginning with finding and evaluating businesses for sale. We discussed several resources, including online platforms, personal networks, and industry-specific channels, to help find potential business opportunities. It's crucial to align these opportunities with your skills, experience, and goals.

We then explored the importance of accurately valuing a business. We outlined methods for deciding whether a business is priced fairly, ensuring that you make informed decisions. After an initial agreement with the seller, the due diligence process (DDI) follows. We covered the DDI's role in verifying key financials, operational details, and contracts to ensure that the business is as presented.

Legal considerations also played a significant role in this chapter. We discussed the difference between buying the legal entity or just the business's assets and the risks associated with each option. Buyers can often minimize liability by opting for an asset purchase agreement (APA), which limits exposure to unknown debts or obligations.

We also touched on negotiating the final purchase price, which can change after completing the DDI. We discussed financing the acquisition through methods like personal savings, loans, or seller financing. Lastly, we outlined how to transition operations smoothly and integrate yourself as the new owner, stressing the importance of communication with stakeholders.

Action Plan

Review the preliminary framework you completed after Chapter 1 and adjust it as required.

Chapter 4
Start or Buy a Franchise

*"Our greatest weakness lies in giving up. The most certain
way to succeed is always to try just one more time" –
Thomas Edison*

Overview

Franchising is an intriguing business entry possibility that deserves close attention. In this chapter, we will examine the various aspects of starting or buying a franchise and how it differs from other methods.

Franchising presents unique opportunities, but it also comes with its own set of challenges. Whether you are looking to open a brand-new franchise or buy an existing one, the details can vary significantly from other entry options. Our focus here will be on understanding the franchise model itself.

To begin, we will discuss how to choose the right franchise. Selecting a franchise that fits your personal and professional goals is crucial to success. We'll explore different options and what factors to consider when making this critical decision.

Evaluating franchise opportunities requires a structured approach. This includes attending discovery days, reviewing systems, examining the franchise's history, and speaking with current franchisees to gain insight into the operations.

Franchise agreements and legal considerations are essential topics when entering a franchise relationship. We will discuss the importance of legal counsel and how to navigate the complexities of these agreements.

Franchising costs and fees can be substantial, and it's important to understand your financial responsibilities. We recommend consulting with an accountant to review these costs before making any commitments.

Another vital step is selecting the right territory for your franchise. A well-chosen location can significantly influence the franchise's success, and we'll cover how to assess and select an ideal territory.

Financing a franchise requires thoughtful planning. We will outline the financing options available and how to approach this critical step in your journey.

Support and training from franchisors play a vital role in a franchise's long-term success. We will explore what kinds of support are typically provided and how to make the most of these resources.

We've previously discussed starting a business from scratch and buying an existing business. While franchising could fall under either category, we will not revisit those points. Instead, this chapter will focus solely on the franchise model and its specific considerations.

Choosing the Right Franchise

Choosing the right franchise begins with understanding how well it fits with your personal and professional goals. Franchising can be a powerful way to enter the business world, but it is crucial to find a match that aligns with your skills, interests, and values. Not every franchise will suit every entrepreneur, so a detailed self-assessment is the first step toward success.

Self-assessment boils down to several principal factors. First, consider your interests. What type of work excites you? The franchise you choose should connect with your passion or at least be an industry you find intriguing. Next, evaluate your skills. What are you good at? Your strengths should complement the demands of the franchise. Values are another significant consideration. The franchise's culture and business model must align with your personal and ethical values.

Think about your ideal lifestyle and work-life balance. Some franchises require long hours or specific commitments, while others may allow for more flexibility. Decide what you want your daily life to look like and choose a franchise that fits this vision. Assessing your financial situation and risk tolerance is also essential. Franchises come with varying levels of investment and risk. Ensure that the financial commitment is something you can manage and that you are comfortable with the associated risks.

After completing your self-assessment, the next step is to consider the sector, industry, and products or services you prefer. Make a list of the industries you are interested in and those you would rather avoid. For example, some people enjoy the food and beverage industry, while others might prefer fitness or education. Narrowing down your sector and industry choices will make your search more focused.

With your list of preferences in hand, it's time to conduct desktop research. Look for franchises that fit your interests, skills, and financial requirements. Investigate their unique selling points, concepts, and advantages. Try to narrow your list to a manageable number of potential franchises to explore further.

Information from franchise associations can be a valuable resource during your research. In the United States, the International Franchise Association (IFA) provides a wealth of information for prospective franchisees. In Canada, the Canadian Franchise Association (CFA) serves a similar purpose, while the British Franchise Association (BFA) does so in the UK. Attending franchise expos is also an excellent way to gather information and meet franchisors in person.

Please refer to Appendix B: Resources for links to franchise associations.

As you continue your research, keep refining your list. The more you investigate, the more apparent it will become which franchises fit your goals and which ones do not. With time, this list will become a targeted set of options that suit your long-term plans.

Evaluating Franchise Opportunities

Once you have narrowed your list of franchise options, the next step is conducting a thorough evaluation of each opportunity. This process involves looking beyond surface-level information and delving deeper into the franchise's inner workings. A well-structured assessment will help you make an informed decision, reducing the chances of unpleasant surprises after you have invested your time and money.

A crucial part of evaluating a franchise is attending a discovery day. This is an event hosted by the franchisor where potential franchisees can meet the company's leadership, learn about the franchise's culture, and get a behind-the-scenes look at operations. Discovery days provide a deeper understanding of what running the franchise will entail.

Most franchisors will invite candidates who have shown genuine interest and passed the first screening process. At these events, expect a detailed overview of the business, including financial projections, marketing strategies, and operational support systems. You can also ask questions directly to the people responsible for the franchise's success. You will likely receive a Franchise Disclosure Document (FDD), which is a legal document provided to potential franchisees outlining essential details such as fees, obligations, and legal requirements.

Next, it's essential to review the franchise systems. The system is the backbone of any franchise, encompassing everything from daily operations to marketing and customer service. You will want to ensure the franchise provides comprehensive training, detailed operational manuals, and ongoing support to help you succeed. Check whether the system has been tested and proven in different markets. A robust system should allow you to replicate the franchisor's business model with minimal friction. If the systems are solid and well-documented, it's a good sign that the franchisor is committed to your success.

Evaluating the franchise's track record is another critical step. Research the franchisor's history, paying close attention to its growth and profitability over time. Has the franchise grown steadily, or has it struggled? Have any legal disputes or financial troubles been reported?

Understanding the franchise's history will give you insight into its long-term viability. Additionally, ask for performance metrics such as average revenue per location, year-on-year growth rates, and franchisee success stories. This data can help you assess whether the franchise is a sound investment.

Current franchisees are one of the most valuable sources of information during this process. Please don't limit your conversations to the franchisees recommended by the franchisor, as they may not provide a complete picture. Instead, reach out to franchisees at random to gain more honest insights. Ask them about their experiences, including the level of support they received, the challenges they faced, and their overall satisfaction with the business. Franchisees are often candid about their experiences, giving you a more realistic perspective on what to expect. Their feedback can also provide clues about potential problems that may not be immediately visible.

To avoid information overload, it's helpful to list the pros and cons of each franchise opportunity. The pros might include strong brand recognition, proven systems, and comprehensive training. The cons could be high initial fees, limited territory availability, or concerns raised by franchisees. Writing down these factors will help you weigh your options objectively and make a balanced decision. Be cautious of franchises that seem to have more red flags than positive points.

By taking a systematic approach to evaluating franchise opportunities, you increase your chances of finding a franchise that fits your personal and financial goals. Remember, the franchisor's business model should be robust, but it also needs to align with your expectations and lifestyle.

Franchise Agreements and Legal Considerations

Franchise agreements are the foundation of any franchise

relationship. This legally binding document outlines the rights and obligations of both the franchisor and the franchisee.

Typically, the agreement covers the duration of the franchise term, the franchisee's responsibilities, ongoing fees, trademark use, territorial rights, and the conditions under which the agreement can be renewed, transferred, or ended. It also specifies what support the franchisor will provide, such as training, marketing, and operational systems.

It is important to note that the franchise agreement is different from the operations manual. While the franchise agreement sets out the legal framework for the relationship, the operations manual provides the day-to-day instructions on how to run the business. The manual typically includes details on marketing strategies, customer service protocols, product offerings, and operational procedures. The two documents work together, but they serve entirely different purposes.

Franchise agreements are often non-negotiable, but there are key terms that prospective franchisees should be aware of. One of the most critical areas to consider is the length of the agreement and the renewal conditions. Some agreements may lock you into long-term commitments without much flexibility, while others provide options for renewal or exit. Another critical factor is the franchise territory.

Ensure that your territory is exclusive and that the franchisor will not open another franchise too close to your location. Also, look out for restrictions on transferring ownership if you ever decide to sell the franchise.

A franchisor should allow you ample time to review the franchise agreement and consult with legal counsel. It is crucial to have an experienced franchise lawyer review the contract before you sign it. Franchise agreements are complex, and without legal advice, you might overlook terms that could be detrimental to your success. Always take the time to understand every aspect of the agreement, and never feel pressured to sign before you are ready.

Legal considerations specific to franchises differ from those for starting a new business or buying an existing one. For example, when buying an existing franchise, you will likely need to sign a new agreement with the franchisor. The terms may not be identical to those of the previous owner, and you will want to ensure that you are receiving the same level of support and training.

Additionally, if you are starting a new franchise, be sure to review the franchisor's obligations to help you establish your location. Some franchisors offer extensive help with site selection and initial marketing, while others provide less assistance.

Franchise laws vary depending on the country or region. In the United States, franchise agreements are governed by the Federal Trade Commission (FTC) and specific state laws. Canada and the UK have their regulations, with the Canadian provinces of Alberta, British Columbia, and Ontario imposing disclosure requirements like those in the U.S. The UK has the British Franchise Association (BFA) to help regulate the industry and protect franchisees.

In conclusion, understanding the franchise agreement is critical to a successful franchise experience. Always seek legal advice and ensure that the agreement aligns with your goals. While the franchise agreement may not cover every operational detail, it defines the legal framework of your relationship with the franchisor, and this should be taken seriously.

Costs and Fees in Franchising

When considering the costs and fees involved in buying a franchise, it's essential to understand that the price tag can vary significantly. However, if you weigh the costs against what you receive in return, buying a franchise isn't necessarily expensive.

Much like paying goodwill when buying an independent business with an established track record, franchise fees often cover valuable assets. These can include comprehensive training, an operations manual, brand recognition, and ongoing support. The franchise system's structure and support can significantly reduce a new business owner's learning curve, making the investment worthwhile.

Even when buying an existing franchise, many of the standard costs and fees are still payable. The new franchisee will still be required to pay ongoing fees to the franchisor, such as royalties and marketing contributions. In addition, some franchisors charge a transfer fee, which is payable when the ownership of an existing franchise changes hands. This ensures that the franchisor continues to provide the same level of support to the new owner.

Initial fee

Franchise costs can be broken into several categories. The first is the initial franchise fee, which grants you the right to operate under the franchisor's brand. This fee can range from a few thousand to hundreds of thousands of dollars, depending on the franchise's brand strength, industry, and location. This fee often includes access to the franchisor's training program, initial marketing efforts, and operations manual.

Next, there are operational costs, which include expenses such as rent, inventory, employee wages, and insurance. In addition, franchisees must cover the cost of their working capital to sustain the business during the initial period when cash flow may be limited.

Ongoing fees

One of the most significant ongoing costs is the royalty fee, which is usually a percentage of your gross sales. Royalties can range from 3% to 10%, depending on the franchise. These fees cover ongoing support from the franchisor, including marketing, product development, and system improvements. Variable fees like royalties are typically calculated based on monthly sales and are payable on a regular basis.

Many franchisors charge both a royalty fee and a separate marketing fee. This marketing fee is also a percentage of sales, often collected in a separate fund. It's used for national and regional marketing efforts to promote the brand and drive customers to individual franchises. While some franchisors may include marketing costs within the royalty fee, many prefer to keep them separate for transparency and to ensure that marketing efforts are focused and effective.

It's important to clarify that fees are likely payable, regardless of whether your business is profitable.

Ad hoc charges and upgrades

In addition to standard fees, some franchises could charge ad hoc marketing fees. These fees are often collected to fund national or regional advertising campaigns. For example, if a franchise runs a statewide promotion, the franchisor may require every franchisee within that state to contribute to the marketing effort.

Franchisees may also face forced upgrades to their facilities. Over time, franchisors may update their branding, product offerings, or customer experience standards. As a result, franchisees could be required to remodel their facilities to stay in line with the new corporate image. These upgrades can be costly, but they are designed to maintain consistency and quality across the franchise network.

To illustrate, let's consider two franchises with vastly different royalty structures. The U.S.-based Anytime Fitness charges a flat rate instead of a percentage. For successful franchisees, this translates into a meager royalty fee.

On the other end of the spectrum, the Canada-based Tim Hortons coffee and fast-food chain charges a royalty fee of 4.5-6% of gross sales and a brand fund fee of 4% of gross sales—a potential total of 10%. Although the fee is steep, it comes with significant brand recognition, extensive marketing support, and a proven system that has been tested in multiple countries.

In conclusion, while the costs and fees associated with franchising can seem daunting, they are often balanced by the benefits you receive. Understanding each fee and its purpose will help you make a more informed decision and manage your financial expectations as a franchisee.

Selecting a Territory

One critical decision when investing in a franchise is selecting the right territory. Most franchise models include some form of territorial limit or protection to avoid oversaturation and ensure that franchisees have enough room to grow their business without direct competition from other franchise locations. This territorial protection can vary depending on the franchise, but it is a crucial part of the franchise agreement.

Franchises use several territorial models, and understanding the differences is essential. Some franchises grant exclusive territories, meaning no other franchise can operate within a defined area. This type of protection can be based on population size, geographic boundaries, or other market factors.

Other franchises may offer semi-exclusive territories, where some overlap between territories is allowed, but the franchisor limits the number of franchisees in the area. Finally, some franchises work on an open territory model, where no specific boundaries exist, and multiple franchises can serve the same market. Each of these models has its pros and cons, so it's essential to understand which one applies to the franchise you are considering.

Choosing a territory is a collaborative process between the prospective franchisee and the franchisor. The franchisor typically provides data on available territories, including demographic information, market trends, and potential for growth. As the prospective franchisee, it is your responsibility to review this data and select a territory that aligns with your business goals and expectations. While the franchisor may offer guidance, the decision largely rests on the franchisee's ability to assess market potential, competition, and local demand.

Once the territory is selected, the next step is choosing the specific location within that territory. This process often involves a combination of market research and guidance from the franchisor. The franchisee typically finds potential locations within the territory, considering factors like foot traffic, visibility, and proximity to competitors. However, in many cases, the franchisor must approve the final location before any lease agreements are signed. This approval process ensures that the area meets the franchisor's standards and is suitable for the brand's image and business model.

In some cases, a franchisee may wish to change their location after they have already established their business. The ability to do this depends on the franchise agreement and the circumstances surrounding the change. If the move is within the same territory, the franchisor will likely need to approve the new location. They will evaluate factors such as whether the move will negatively affect other franchisees or disrupt the market. On the other hand, if the move involves transferring to a new territory, the process becomes more complicated, as the franchisee will need to negotiate new territorial rights. In either scenario, both the franchisee and franchisor must collaborate closely to ensure that the business can continue to operate successfully in its new location.

In conclusion, selecting a territory and choosing a location are critical steps in establishing a successful franchise. Both processes require careful collaboration between the franchisee and franchisor, ensuring that the territory offers room for growth and that the location is optimized for the brand's success. Understanding the roles of each party and the protections provided by the franchise agreement will help guide you toward making the best decision for your business.

Financing the Franchise

Financing a franchise is, in many ways, similar to funding a start-up or the acquisition of an existing business. Whether you're purchasing a new or established franchise, the basic principles of financing apply. Lenders will expect to see a solid financial plan, evidence of market demand, and a clear understanding of the business model before approving any loans. However, there are unique advantages to financing a franchise that can make securing funds a little easier, especially when dealing with well-established brands.

One of the essential requirements for financing any business, including a franchise, is the business plan. Just as with any start-up, financiers will likely expect a detailed business plan outlining your financial projections, marketing strategies, and operational goals. In the case of a franchise, your plan should also include information on the franchise's history, support systems, and expected performance based on similar franchise locations. A comprehensive plan gives lenders confidence that you have a clear path to profitability.

A significant advantage of financing a well-established franchise is the proven history it provides. Established franchises come with a successful business model that has been replicated across multiple locations. This track record offers a level of comfort to financiers, as it reduces the perceived risk compared to starting an independent business from scratch. The more successful the franchise, the easier it becomes to convince lenders that your business is likely to succeed. Franchises with recognizable brand names and dedicated support systems offer built-in stability that financiers find attractive.

In some cases, specialist financiers or boutique firms have developed strong relationships with prominent franchise brands. These financiers have in-depth knowledge of the franchise's operations and a direct line of communication with key personnel. Because they specialize in franchise lending, they are often more comfortable offering loans to prospective franchisees, as they can better evaluate the risks involved. Their familiarity with the franchise's performance data, training programs, and marketing strategies reduces the guesswork and increases their confidence in extending credit.

In scenarios where franchise-specific financiers are involved, the franchisor may play a significant role in easing the process. Many franchisors maintain relationships with lenders who specialize in franchise financing and can introduce prospective franchisees to these lenders. By making the introduction, the franchisor helps streamline the financing process, reducing the time and effort needed for the franchisee to secure funds. These relationships benefit both parties, as the financier gains a qualified borrower, and the franchisee gains access to specialized lending services.

In conclusion, financing a franchise follows many of the same principles as funding other business ventures, but the advantages of an established franchise model can make the process smoother. Lenders are more likely to finance a franchise with a proven track record, and boutique lenders specializing in franchises can offer added support. With the franchisor's involvement in the process, securing financing can become even more efficient.

Training and Support from Franchisors

One of the biggest reasons entrepreneurs consider buying into a franchise is the comprehensive training and ongoing support that comes with it. This support, condensed into an operations manual, is designed to guide franchisees through every aspect of running their business.

Unlike starting a business independently, where you learn by trial and error, a franchise provides you with proven systems and processes from day one. This advantage significantly reduces the learning curve and increases the likelihood of success.

Training typically starts at the franchisor's headquarters, where new franchisees receive instruction on everything from daily operations to customer service. This initial training often includes workshops, lectures, and firsthand experience to ensure franchisees understand the brand's systems. After the training at headquarters, franchisees might spend time at existing franchise locations. This allows them to see how the business works in real life, giving them a clearer picture of what to expect when they open their location.

Franchisors also offer support for setting up the new location. This can include help with site selection, negotiating leases, and designing the business's layout. Franchisors often have preferred suppliers and contractors, which can streamline the setup process and ensure that the location meets the brand's standards. This support extends to the operational phase as well, covering day-to-day management, staffing, and inventory management.

Marketing support is another critical aspect of the franchisor's role. Before a location opens, franchisors usually provide marketing materials and strategies to generate buzz around the new franchise. Whether it's social media campaigns, direct mailers, or community events, the franchisor's goal is to drive traffic to the new location from day one. Once the business is up and running, the franchisor offers ongoing support, which may include regular check-ins, training updates, and access to an online portal where franchisees can find resources, tips, and advice. Head office support is always available to help franchisees navigate challenges or improve performance.

One interesting example of long franchisee training comes from McDonald's, where the training program can last up to 12 months (part-time), depending on the franchisee's background and experience. During this period, not only the franchisee but also key management and some staff undergo extensive training.

McDonald's makes sure its franchisees are fully prepared to run the business by the time their store opens. This commitment to comprehensive training is one of the reasons McDonald's maintains such exacting standards across all its locations.

The sheer volume of information in the operations manual can be staggering. For instance, Subway's operations manual is reportedly over 500 pages long. This manual covers everything from food preparation and customer service to financial management and marketing. Such detailed guidance ensures that every aspect of the business is standardized and follows the franchisor's guidelines, contributing to the uniformity of service and product quality across all franchise locations.

Franchisors also conduct routine inspections to ensure that franchisees are adhering to brand standards. These inspections might focus on cleanliness, product quality, customer service, or overall operations. In addition, many franchisors employ "mystery shoppers"—individuals who visit the franchise posing as regular customers but who report back to the franchisor on their experience. This helps franchisors check franchisees' performance from a customer's perspective, identifying areas that may need improvement. The mystery shopper reports are often used as a tool to provide more training or make necessary adjustments to maintain the brand's reputation.

In summary, franchisors' training and support are crucial to a franchise's success. The initial training helps new franchisees hit the ground running, while the ongoing backing ensures they stay on track. With resources like a comprehensive operations manual and inspections, franchisors provide the structure needed to run a successful business. This support system is often the biggest advantage of owning a franchise, making it an attractive option for entrepreneurs.

Chapter Recap

In this chapter, we explored the unique aspects of starting or buying a franchise and offered detailed insights into the franchising model. We began by discussing how to choose the right franchise, emphasizing the importance of aligning personal goals, skills, and values with the franchise model. Self-assessment, research, and franchise associations were highlighted as critical steps in narrowing down options.

Next, we examined evaluating franchise opportunities, stressing the value of attending discovery days and reviewing franchise systems and track records. Speaking with current franchisees to gain practical insights was also recommended, alongside documenting the pros and cons to avoid information overload.

We then delved into franchise agreements and legal considerations, explaining vital elements like the duration of agreements, territorial rights, and the importance of seeking legal counsel. We also covered the difference between the legal framework of the agreement and the manual's day-to-day operational guidance.

In the section on costs and fees in franchising, we explored the financial obligations, from initial franchise fees to royalties and marketing contributions. We emphasized the role of accountants in reviewing these fees and understanding the financial commitment.

We further covered selecting a territory, explaining how franchisees and franchisors collaborate in choosing territories and locations while maintaining brand standards. Financing a franchise was another focus, where we highlighted how franchisee-specific lenders can facilitate financing through solid relationships with franchisors.

Finally, we discussed the training and support provided by franchisors, illustrating the importance of initial and ongoing assistance, using examples of extensive training programs and comprehensive operations manuals.

Action plan

Review the preliminary framework you completed after Chapter 1 and adjust it as required.

Chapter 5
Case Studies of Real-Life Examples

"And the day came when the risk to remain tight in a bud was more painful than the risk it took to blossom" – Anaïs Nin

Overview

This chapter provides real-life case studies that highlight diverse business entry methods. We will explore the experiences of four entrepreneurs, focusing on their successes and challenges. Names have been changed to ensure their privacy, but the lessons shared are genuine and instructive.

The first case study details the journey of a married couple who started a service-based business. With limited capital but good industry knowledge, they navigated the complexities of building a service company from scratch.

We will examine the strategies they used to get customers, differentiate their services, and sustain growth over time. Their story highlights how adaptability and customer focus are crucial in service industries.

Next, we present the case of a manufacturing startup. Unlike service businesses, this venture required significant upfront investment in equipment and production facilities. The entrepreneur faced challenges like managing operational costs and creating efficient workflows. This case will show the importance of careful financial planning, supplier management, and quality control in a manufacturing context.

The third story features another couple who initially bought a franchise and eventually sold it at a small profit. Motivated by their positive experience, they reinvested in the same franchise but in a different location.

Their journey shows how leveraging brand recognition and operational support can lead to repeated success, provided the market and location are well-researched. We will also discuss the decision-making process behind choosing the new location and how their past experiences helped improve outcomes.

Our final case study involves a franchise failure. This entrepreneur entered a franchise agreement without conducting thorough due diligence. Poor site selection, lack of local market understanding, and inadequate franchisor support led to the business's eventual closure. Analyzing this failure will provide insight into the potential pitfalls of franchising, emphasizing the need for careful evaluation before commitment.

To conclude, we will summarize the key lessons learned from these case studies. Whether starting from nothing, buying into a franchise, or expanding to new locations, success requires a combination of market research, financial prudence, and strategic planning.

Readers will understand the importance of aligning business choices with personal skills and the broader market environment.

Case Study 1: Starting a Service Business

"Building Frames, Building Dreams: The Story of Phillip and Victoria's Service Business"

Phillip's Career Start

After qualifying as a cabinetmaker from trade school, Phillip landed a job at a new picture mold manufacturer. He enjoyed the productive environment, watching as large chunks of wood transformed into beautiful molds. The industrial side of production fascinated him. Phillip's eagerness to learn helped him progress quickly, and he was soon offered a role as a sales representative. Coming from a humble background, he saw this as an opportunity to increase his earnings. He also believed his entrepreneurial mindset would help him excel in sales. He was right—Phillip successfully built a substantial client base of picture-framing businesses.

Victoria's Aspirations

Meanwhile, Phillip's wife, Victoria, was working as a graphic designer. She dreamed of one day using her artistic talents to work in interior design, a subject that fascinated her deeply. Together, Phillip and Victoria worked hard and saved enough to buy their first home. The house was modest, located in a tranquil suburban community. The neighborhood had a mix of modern and traditional homes and was known for its family-friendly atmosphere and excellent schools. Most of the residents were professionals in white-collar jobs. The suburb also offered parks, shopping centers, and local restaurants, making it an ideal place for a young couple.

Phillip's Job Insecurity

Not long after Phillip was promoted to sales representative, his employer began showing signs of financial stress. Worried that the company might close and leave him jobless, Phillip decided to think ahead. They had only a small amount of savings, and he knew he needed to act before it was too late. As he traveled from one client to another, Phillip began considering starting his own business. He knew the picture framing industry well—at least, he thought he did.

The Honest Conversation

Phillip shared his idea with Victoria, and she became excited at the possibility. However, after an honest conversation, they realized their limitations. Phillip had practical knowledge of the products and strong sales and people skills. However, he lacked artistic flair and had no experience managing a business. Victoria, on the other hand, had little knowledge of the products but good artistic intuition. She also learned some basic business management skills while acting as the office manager at an advertising agency.

Market Research and Preparations

After a week of discussions, they decided to take the plunge while keeping their jobs as long as possible. Phillip would gauge the market potential in their suburb. He also began looking for suppliers, focusing on quality picture molds, since he could not rely on his current employer for support. Meanwhile, Victoria enrolled in a short, part-time business management course with a focus on bookkeeping. She also started looking for a suitable space for their business.

Writing a Business Plan

Together, Phillip and Victoria worked through the challenges of writing a business plan. Phillip used his industry connections and knowledge to find a well-established mold supplier willing to grant a 30-day credit facility and weekly deliveries.

However, they needed cash to buy equipment and shop fittings. They found a small shop in a busy strip mall, but the landlord required a significant deposit, given their inexperience. With their savings unable to cover all expenses, they borrowed money from family members.

Though more was needed, they used it as their own contribution when approaching their bank for a loan. With no equity available in their house, they relied on their impeccable history with their bank accounts, which helped sway the loan officer to approve a small loan.

Opening the Business

Three months later, they opened their shop. They did a fantastic job with the shop layout and display, creating a welcoming atmosphere. However, their initial enthusiasm quickly turned to worry when they realized clients were not lining up to get their items framed. The importance of marketing, which they had neglected, became painfully apparent.

Marketing Efforts Begin

Determined to make their business work, Phillip and Victoria began executing various marketing initiatives. Phillip visited large firms offering corporate discounts to their employees. He also put up pamphlets at colleges and schools, focusing on those that issued certificates. His people skills helped him make meaningful connections, generating a small trickle of clients. Back at the shop, Victoria began an email campaign to introduce their services to the community. She contacted interior decorators and make-over specialists to an open house event to introduce their offerings. As they completed their first framing orders, she effectively used social media to flaunt their work.

Challenges in Reaching Breakeven

It took them five months to reach breakeven. Starting their marketing late put significant pressure on their cash flow, as they had just enough capital according to their plan, with no backup funds. Despite the challenges, they managed to keep their overheads low. By working prudently with their budget and maintaining expenses steady, they began to see the results of their efforts.

Growth and Expansion

Exactly two years after opening their first shop, they managed to expand by opening a second business in a neighboring suburb. They hired an experienced woman to manage the new location. The commute between the two shops was manageable, allowing Phillip and Victoria to take turns visiting the new location each day. This helped ensure that their original systems were followed precisely and allowed them to take advantage of economies of scale. Phillip could move molds between the two shops within hours if needed, ensuring smooth operations.

Improving Quality of Life

Once both businesses were profitable, Phillip and Victoria found ways to improve their quality of life without harming the business. Given their client profile, they decided to adjust their working hours. They opened at 11:00 AM and closed at 5:00 PM on weekdays, with shorter hours on Saturdays. Before making this change, they used social media extensively to inform their clients. Their quality of work was so high that clients accepted the adjusted hours without complaint.

Key Takeaways

Phillip and Victoria had complementary strengths that helped their business succeed. Phillip's industry knowledge and sales skills, combined with Victoria's artistic intuition and business management basics, made them a solid team. Their weaknesses were primarily in marketing, which they should have planned and executed earlier. Two prominent learning points emerged from their journey: the need to start marketing efforts early and the value of persistence and adaptability in business.

Conclusion

Phillip summarized their journey well when he said, "In our next venture, whatever that may be, I will start planning the marketing the very moment we decide to start that venture!"

This case study confirms the old saying: an energetic and determined entrepreneur with a flawed plan will likely trump a mediocre or unmotivated entrepreneur with a good plan. Phillip and Victoria's journey was marked by enthusiasm, hard work, and adaptation—qualities that eventually led them to success.

Case Study 2: Starting a Manufacturing Business

"Forged Through Fire: The Journey of a Manufacturing Startup"

A Corporate Nightmare Sparks New Dreams

Adrian and his colleagues had dedicated years to working for a national paper and packaging company. They specialized in the corrugated division, a highly profitable unit. Everything changed when the company was sold to another national conglomerate, triggering a nightmare that none of them anticipated. The merger brought conflicts at the management level. Tensions arose, decision-making processes dragged on, and the once smooth workflow became chaotic. Eventually, two of the four colleagues were retrenched, and the other two were left in a toxic work environment where every day felt like a battle for survival.

The Realization

After many sleepless nights and stressful days, Adrian and his three colleagues found themselves questioning their future. They had all grown unhappy and realized that they had the skills to start their own venture. Adrian, being an accountant, had all the financial skills needed, including knowledge specific to the corrugated industry. The rest of the team brought expertise in three other essential functions: production management, sales, and supply chain coordination. They had the entire package needed to start a corrugated manufacturing company.

Pooling Resources and Planning

The four decided to pull their resources and create a company together. They agreed on shareholding based on each member's contribution and role in the company. Writing a business plan proved more manageable than they expected. With their collective experience, they knew the industry inside out and had access to the information they needed. They worked seamlessly together to craft a plan that covered all aspects, from production to sales and risk management.

The Funding Hurdle

However, crafting a plan was just the beginning. They needed more funds to bring their vision to life. Adrian was the only one with equity in his house and some savings. The others had limited savings but needed more to make a substantial contribution. Their only choice was to approach a viability-based financier since they needed more collateral to offer a conventional lender. The financier saw the quality of their application, especially considering the team's collective experience, and recognized the opportunity. However, they were cautious about the risk and insisted on taking a 30% equity stake in the business.

A Creative Solution

This nearly derailed the entire negotiation. None of the team members were interested in diluting their ownership. Adrian, with his financial acumen, proposed an alternative. He suggested offering the financier a small royalty percentage on sales for the term of the loan. This would compensate the financier for the risk while keeping equity intact. For the team, a royalty would be a variable expense instead of a fixed one. If the company became wildly successful, both parties would benefit—the financier from the royalties and the team from paying off the loan quicker, thus ending the royalties. This creative solution worked, and the deal was approved.

The Struggles Begin

Despite their knowledge and experience, the team quickly realized the difference between running their own business and working in a large corporation. They no longer had corporate muscle behind them. Finding and securing the heavy equipment took longer than expected, and they could not secure the beneficial pricing they had hoped for. The only suitable industrial premises they found were just large enough to reach breakeven but offered little room for growth. Despite the limitation, they reasoned that it was better to grow out of space than to have too much idle space without growth.

Commissioning Challenges

The commissioning of the plant and equipment proved to be far trickier than they had expected. The process dragged on, eating into their precious working capital. There were moments of intense frustration as delays mounted and bills piled up. Yet, the team pushed forward, determined to see their dream become a reality.

Early Success and Cash Flow Tightrope

Once everything was finally in place, they secured their first orders. With competitive pricing and short lead times, sales began to pick up quickly. In fact, sales grew faster than they had expected, and they soon faced a new challenge: cash flow.

They managed to secure large and stable clients, but these clients demanded 45 to 60-day credit terms. Meanwhile, their suppliers only allowed them 30 to 45 days, creating a constant struggle to balance inflows and outflows. Adrian found himself walking a tightrope every day, trying to manage cash flow and keep the business running smoothly.

Growth Creates Pressure

The rapid growth in sales also meant that they needed to carry ever-larger inventories of corrugated sheets. This, in turn, worsened the cash flow situation, as more cash was tied up in stock. The limited space in their facility added to the pressure. They needed to expand, but moving to a new location would mean at least a month-long disruption in production. Such a move could jeopardize their business and their clients' confidence. Despite these challenges, the team remained optimistic. The issues they faced were the result of growth, not failure.

A Fortunate Break

Luck was on their side when the neighboring industrial building became available. The tenant had gone bankrupt, and the landlord was eager to find a new occupant. He offered them a favorable rental deal with a relatively small deposit compared to industry standards. With the space issue solved, Adrian saw a new opportunity.

To address the cash flow challenge, they could add a four-hour shift to their existing nine-hour shift. Adrian negotiated with their major suppliers, convincing them to extend credit terms to 60 days in exchange for higher purchasing volumes.

Resistance from Within

Manufacturing employees welcomed the overtime opportunity, and management promised to recruit more workers as soon as possible to alleviate the workload. However, two of the founding team members balked at the idea of longer hours.

Even though they were in managerial positions and could rely on supervisors in their absence, they were not keen on putting in extra time. Tensions rose, and a walkout seemed imminent—the lack of dividends added fuel to the fire. Although the business was profitable and growing, cash flow constraints meant no dividends could be paid yet. Adrian was firm in his stance—employees and the business had to come first before shareholders could benefit.

Facilitating a Solution

Realizing the gravity of the situation, Adrian reached out to their original financier. He had developed an excellent working relationship with the relationship manager, who agreed to act as a facilitator. After briefing the relationship manager on all the details, a meeting was held to address the concerns. Emotions ran high during the discussion, but eventually, everyone came on board. They understood that the path ahead would require hard work and that delayed gratification was necessary for long-term success. The entire team agreed to the extended work hours with a renewed sense of commitment.

Five Years Later

Fast forward five years and the business is a resounding success. They have achieved year-on-year growth and repaid their loan, putting an end to the royalties. Systems and processes are now well-oiled, and the plant runs two full shifts every day of the week.

The hard work and sacrifices have paid off, and the business now pays handsome dividends, rewarding the team for its resilience and tenacity.

Key Takeaways

Adrian and his colleagues' journey was an emotional rollercoaster filled with moments of doubt, determination, and triumph. They navigated through corporate conflicts, funding challenges, cash flow crises, and internal disagreements, but their belief in their vision kept them going. Their story illustrates that entrepreneurship is not for the faint of heart—it requires creativity, resilience, and the ability to adapt to ever-changing circumstances.

Case Study 3: Franchise Ownership

"Turning the Tables: Henry's Journey to Franchise Success"

Turning a Struggling Franchise Around

This story takes us to Gauteng, South Africa—the smallest province by land area but the most economically significant. Henry, an unassuming but energetic entrepreneur, bought an underperforming franchise restaurant several years ago.

The franchise was in poor shape, with several problems: a run-down location in a suburban CBD suffering from urban blight, outdated décor, and an incompetent owner. The franchise was on the verge of closing. But Henry saw an opportunity and convinced the franchisor to give him a chance. Given

Henry's strong hospitality and food experience, the franchisor agreed. They preferred to give up some initial fees rather than close the franchise, which could harm the overall brand. So, they removed the struggling franchisee in accordance with the franchise agreement, and Henry bought the franchise for a reduced fee.

Taking a Calculated Risk

Henry knew that buying a struggling business was generally not advisable. But he backed himself. He saw this as a chance to prove his abilities while gaining entry at a lower cost. And being single, he could afford to put in the long hours needed without the pressures that come with a family. It wasn't just Henry's effort that mattered—it was a team effort. Henry worked tirelessly on every aspect of the business while the franchisor provided eager support and was keen to see the franchise turn around. The teamwork paid off, and eventually, the franchise became profitable.

Settling into a Comfortable Routine

With the business finally making money, Henry could revert to regular working hours. One aspect of the restaurant that he particularly enjoyed was the operating hours. The restaurant was not open during the evenings, making it different from many other restaurants.

Although the restaurant opened seven days a week, its peak business hours were breakfast, brunch, and lunch. The restaurant closed by mid-afternoon, giving Henry the work-life balance he wanted—running his own business while still having time to pursue his interests.

Wanting More

However, even though the restaurant was profitable, it eventually reached a peak and then stagnated. Henry wanted more. The location was part of the problem, and neither he nor the franchisor was interested in making costly upgrades. The CBD had not recovered from its decay, and they both knew it was not worth the investment.

A New Opportunity Emerges

Around that time, an unexpected opportunity arose. In a nearby city, a new development was in the works. Authorities had approved the redevelopment of an old, abandoned drive-in theater into a strip mall. The mall was situated next to a prominent highway, with visible and easily accessible on- and off-ramps. It was a prime location, and the franchisor had secured the rights to establish a restaurant as part of the mall's tenant mix. Henry heard about the development before construction had even begun. He immediately approached the franchisor, eager to seize the opportunity.

Negotiations with the Franchisor

Henry's track record with the struggling franchise spoke volumes about his capabilities. The franchisor was more than willing to discuss the new opportunity with him. But that still left the question of what to do with the now profitable yet outdated franchise. The franchisor acknowledged that the current location was no longer suitable and did not meet their standards. They both understood that finding a new franchisee was unlikely, if not impossible. Henry could not sell it as a franchise, but they both agreed that closing the restaurant would be detrimental to everyone involved.

An Unexpected Solution

The answer came from another business owner. This person owned several low-cost takeaway businesses and was interested in the location. He found it suitable and was willing to use most of the existing equipment. With minimal cost, he could change the interior to fit his preferred takeaway setup. Rebranding the business would also be easy. By keeping the existing color scheme and making strategic changes to the names and logos, he could avoid reinventing the wheel. Henry and the franchisor reached an agreement with the takeaway entrepreneur. The franchisor lost potential fees and royalties, and Henry accepted a lower sale price than he might have hoped for. However, both parties recognized the bigger picture and the opportunity ahead.

A Welcome Break and New Preparations

With the existing business de-franchised and sold, Henry had time to enjoy a well-earned break. He also had time to prepare for his next venture. The new mall would take 12 months to complete, giving him ample time to put together a comprehensive business plan. Being single and a careful spender, Henry had managed to accumulate enough savings and assets to use as collateral. Between his personal assets and the commercial kitchen equipment of the new business, Henry was able to offer sufficient collateral to secure a loan. This allowed him to approach multiple lenders and negotiate the best possible terms.

Opening the New Franchise

The mall opened on schedule, and the restaurant was one of

the first businesses to open its doors. In large part, things went according to plan, thanks to Henry's earlier hard work and determination.

However, tenant uptake in the mall was well below expectations. Many retail spaces remained empty, which led to significantly less foot traffic than expected. This situation was potentially devastating for Henry. But two key factors helped him pull through. First, the franchise brand enjoyed strong recognition and popularity. Clients were willing to travel to the restaurant for breakfast and lunch, which meant he did not have to rely solely on passing foot traffic. Second, the mall was in a growing suburban area with a substantial number of middle- to high-income residents. These clients often visited the restaurant, even if they had no other business in the mall.

Top-Notch Service and Quality

On top of brand recognition, Henry ensured that his service and food quality were top-notch. This commitment to excellence led to satisfied clients and repeat business. The restaurant became a popular spot for locals, and word of mouth began to spread. Slowly but surely, the empty retail spaces in the mall began to fill up, and foot traffic increased. Henry's hard work and dedication were finally paying off. The journey had not been easy, but his resilience was a critical factor in overcoming the obstacles he faced.

A Collaborative Success

The success of the new franchise was a testament to the robust support from the franchisor and Henry's determination as an entrepreneur. They worked together to overcome the challenges of an outdated franchise, the struggles of waiting for a new development, and the difficulties of opening in a mall with low initial occupancy. Henry's story is a prime example of how a strong franchise network, combined with a knowledgeable and tenacious entrepreneur, can lead to a successful business.

Key Takeaways

Henry's journey was filled with ups and downs. He took a significant risk in buying an underperforming franchise, but his dedication and hard work turned it into a success. When faced with stagnation, he did not settle but sought new opportunities. His willingness to compromise when selling the old franchise, combined with his preparedness for the new venture, demonstrated his long-term vision. The challenges of low tenant uptake in the new mall tested his resilience, but he pushed through by leveraging the brand's strength and focusing on quality and service.

Case Study 4: An Acquisition Gone Wrong

"A Risky Gamble - When Ambition Overpowers Reality"

Introduction

This is the story of a well-established family business that ended up in the hands of an ambitious but inexperienced new owner. It highlights how an acquisition, which appeared ideal at first glance, can fall apart due to missteps and poor judgment. The pre-cast concrete fencing business started in the U.S. Midwest, was built from scratch by a father determined to create a better future for his family. It provided not only a livelihood but also a bond for his children—his daughter and two sons—all of whom worked in the business. A quintessential family endeavor, it catered primarily to domestic clients and occasionally accepted larger corporate contracts if they fit within its capacity. However, a series of events ultimately led to its demise, highlighting the perils of inexperience, poor financial planning, and unrealistic expectations.

Building the Dream

The business was founded by a father who had a dream of giving his family a stable and prosperous future. He invested all his energy and resources into building a pre-cast concrete fencing company from the ground up. From the very beginning, he focused on delivering quality products and keeping his customers happy. With a fifty-mile service radius, he kept the domestic customers satisfied while staying disciplined enough to turn down mega contracts. This self-restraint ensured that the business could continue to serve its local clientele without compromising quality.

The father's three children worked side by side with him. The daughter managed sales and customer relations, while the sons took charge of manufacturing and logistics. Together, they built an ideal family business. They were well-known in their community for the high quality of their products and their reliability. The father often took pride in the fact that he managed to turn a small venture into a sustainable, profitable business that could one day be handed over to the next generation.

Family Tensions Surface

As the father approached retirement age, he believed he had a clear plan for handing over the reins to his children. He envisioned the three siblings taking over the business together, dividing responsibilities according to their skills. To him, it was a perfect solution that would keep the business in the family and secure their future.

However, the family discussion about succession took an unexpected turn. It quickly escalated into a bitter argument about titles and reporting lines. Each sibling had their own vision of what their role should be, and none of them were willing to compromise. The conflict became so heated that the daughter decided to leave at once. Feeling deeply disappointed and fed up with the infighting, the father decided to sell the business instead. His dream of a peaceful handover had shattered, and he no longer had the patience to deal with the turmoil.

The Introduction of Richard

Determined to sell the business, the owner approached a local small business training center. He casually mentioned the sale to the office manager, Richard, and left behind a one-page overview of the business. Richard, a young and enthusiastic individual, had always wanted to own a business. He had spent years getting theoretical knowledge in management and was just waiting for the right opportunity.

However, Richard made his first mistake when he jumped at the opportunity without thoroughly considering whether this type of business suited him. He had no practical business experience and lacked technical skills—two crucial elements for running a manufacturing business. However, he was blinded by his desire to become an entrepreneur and was convinced that his theoretical knowledge was enough.

The Deal Takes Shape

Richard contacted the owner and expressed his interest in buying the business. After the first meeting, Richard was given an overview of the operations and some financial details. The company seemed solid, with a good track record of profits. Richard was eager to go ahead, even though he lacked the resources to finance the acquisition.

With limited savings and no collateral, Richard's only workable option was seller financing. He convinced his bank to give him a personal line of credit, and with this, combined with his savings, he managed to offer the seller almost 20% of the purchase price. However, this figure was misleading—it consisted of only 6% of his funds, with the rest borrowed from the bank. Richard pushed himself to offer the largest monthly payment he could afford, hoping to secure the deal. The seller, who was tired of family drama and eager to move on, accepted Richard's terms.

Red Flags Ignored

The structure of the financing was Richard's second major mistake. Most financiers agree that a minimum of 20% in personal contribution is needed for a prudent gearing structure. Richard's debt-to-equity ratio was a significant red flag that he chose to ignore. He had the theoretical knowledge to recognize the risk but lacked the discipline to apply best practices in this real-world scenario.

Before finalizing the sale, the seller invited Richard to work alongside him for a few days to get a feel for the business. Richard enjoyed those days and was excited about taking over. They agreed on a three-month handover period, with the seller remaining available for an additional three months in a standby capacity.

Richard made his third mistake by opting not to hire legal counsel for the purchase agreement. Instead, he used a contract template from a friend to save money. The agreement lacked a crucial suspensive clause that would have made the deal contingent on a satisfactory due diligence investigation (DDI). After spending just three days with the seller, Richard felt confident enough to go ahead without conducting a formal DDI. This haphazard approach meant that he remained unaware of the actual condition of the plant and equipment.

The Handover and Early Challenges

With the deal finalized, Richard became the new owner. From the very beginning, he faced the challenge of replacing the seller's two sons, who had managed the manufacturing and logistics aspects of the business. This was Richard's fourth mistake. Losing key personnel meant that Richard had to find and train new employees while simultaneously trying to learn every aspect of the business himself.

Despite these early challenges, the business initially performed according to expectations. Sales remained steady, and Richard managed to maintain profit margins. After some time, he successfully replaced the two sons, and it seemed like things were beginning to stabilize. However, Richard's lack of technical ability and experience would soon prove to be a significant liability.

The First Major Setback

Nine months into his ownership, the business faced its first major crisis. The most critical piece of equipment—the concrete batching plant—broke down. By this time, the seller was no longer available to offer advice, and Richard lacked the technical knowledge to diagnose the problem. He had to rely entirely on external mechanics, who took longer than expected to find and fix the issue.

What could have been a simple fix, routinely handled by the previous owner and his sons, turned into a prolonged and costly repair. The extended downtime caused significant disruption to production, resulting in lost revenue. To cover the repair costs, Richard was forced to skip a payment to the seller. The tight financial situation was worsened by the high monthly payments that Richard had committed to—leaving no room for unexpected expenses.

The Harsh Winter

The second major challenge came during Richard's second winter as the business owner. The company typically experienced a minor seasonal slowdown during mid-winter, but this year was different. One of the harshest winters in decades brought operations to a complete halt for five weeks. No manufacturing could take place, and installation projects had to be postponed. With no income during this period, Richard was unable to make another payment to the seller.

Richard's lack of financial resilience became painfully clear. His highly leveraged position and excessive monthly payments left no buffer for dealing with seasonal fluctuations. Despite his intelligence and willingness to learn, Richard's poor financial planning had put the business in a precarious position.

A Fatal Flaw

For all his knowledge and hard work, Richard had a fatal

personality flaw—his spending habits. He believed that business ownership entitled him to a luxurious lifestyle. While he managed the business strictly according to a budget, he spent lavishly on himself. He did not understand that ownership, in and by itself, is meaningless without sustainable profits to support it.

Richard's inability to control his spending drained the business's limited financial resources. Instead of reinvesting profits into maintaining and improving operations, he diverted funds for his own benefit. This lack of discipline ultimately pushed the business to the brink.

The Final Blow

By the time Richard reached his second anniversary as the owner, the situation had become dire. The seller, frustrated by missed payments and broken promises, issued a legal demand for the total outstanding amount of the private loan. Without the ability to pay and with the seller unwilling to negotiate further, Richard faced asset seizure and the eventual closure of the business.

The dream of business ownership that Richard had chased turned into a nightmare. The lack of proper planning, failure to conduct due diligence, over-leveraging, loss of key personnel, and personal financial mismanagement all contributed to the downfall of a once-thriving family business.

Key Takeaways

This case serves as a classic example of how not to buy a business. Richard's story is a cautionary tale about the importance of thorough self-assessment before pursuing an acquisition. Theoretical knowledge alone is insufficient—practical experience, financial discipline, and technical skills are also essential.

Richard's ambition to become a business owner blinded him to the realities of the situation. Despite the opportunities that the business offered, his lack of preparation and poor financial decisions led to failure. This case study underscores the need for a balanced approach—combining ambition with caution, theoretical knowledge with practical skills, and financial risk with sound planning.

Chapter Recap

The case studies presented reveal important lessons for aspiring entrepreneurs and business owners. One key lesson is the need for adaptability and perseverance in the face of challenges. In each story, the entrepreneurs had to make tough decisions, learn new skills, and overcome setbacks. Phillip and Victoria demonstrated adaptability when their marketing efforts initially fell short—they quickly adjusted their approach to ensure their business's survival. Similarly, Adrian and his team showed perseverance as they navigated cash flow issues and internal disagreements.

Another critical lesson is the importance of financial planning and discipline. Financial mismanagement can lead to catastrophic consequences, as seen in Richard's case. Adrian's success, on the other hand, came partly from his creative approach to funding and his ability to manage cash flow effectively. Business owners must be prepared for potential disruptions, such as equipment failures or seasonal downturns, and should maintain a financial buffer to withstand these challenges.

The case studies also emphasize the importance of aligning personal skills with business choices. Richard's failure was mainly due to his lack of technical skills and experience, which proved detrimental when faced with unexpected challenges. Entrepreneurs need to assess their strengths and weaknesses realistically before embarking on a venture, ensuring that they are well-equipped to handle the demands of their chosen path.

Common Pitfalls

A common pitfall seen in these case studies is the need for proper market research and planning. In the first case, Phillip and Victoria were initially caught off guard by the lack of clients, which could have been avoided with better market research and a solid marketing plan before launching their business. Market research is crucial for understanding the target audience, the competitive landscape, and potential challenges.

Another pitfall is inadequate due diligence during an acquisition. Richard's decision to forego a formal due diligence investigation led to disastrous consequences. Due diligence provides a comprehensive understanding of a business's financial health, operational status, and potential risks. Without it, an entrepreneur may inherit hidden problems, such as outdated equipment or financial liabilities, which can jeopardize the entire venture. Cutting corners during the acquisition process, as Richard did, is a critical mistake that can lead to failure.

Financial over-leverage is also a significant pitfall. Richard's highly leveraged position, with minimal personal contribution and excessive debt, left him vulnerable to even minor setbacks. High monthly payments to the seller, combined with unexpected downtime, pushed the business into financial instability. Entrepreneurs should avoid over-leveraging and instead aim for a prudent debt-to-equity ratio, allowing room for unforeseen expenses and downturns.

Lastly, a flawed perception of business ownership can also lead to failure. Richard's belief that ownership entitled him to a luxurious lifestyle ultimately drained the company's resources. Business owners must understand that profits must be reinvested in the business to ensure long-term growth and stability. Personal spending should be kept separate from business finances, especially during the early stages when the business is vulnerable. Failure to maintain financial discipline, as seen in Richard's case, can lead to business closure and significant personal losses.

Action Plan

Review the preliminary framework you completed after Chapter 1 and adjust it according to the lessons learned and common pitfalls discussed in this chapter.

Chapter 6
Making the Decision

*"Every decision brings with it some good, some bad, some
lessons, and some luck. The only thing that's for sure is
that indecision steals many years from many people who
wind up wishing they'd just had the courage to leap"– Doe
Zantamata*

Overview

We are now at a pivotal point in this book, exploring the
culmination of different business entry methods discussed
so far. In earlier chapters, we've examined the potential of starting
a business, buying an existing one, entering a franchise, and
learning from real-life examples.

Each chapter offered detailed insights into the opportunities,
challenges, and considerations associated with these different
routes. Chapter 6 will take us a step further by integrating these
options with your personal goals and creating a framework to
guide you toward the best decision.

This chapter aims to help you align what you've learned with your
unique circumstances. Once you have a clear understanding of
which entry method aligns best with your needs, the next step is
creating a decision-making framework. This framework will serve

as a structured guide to weigh your options systematically, using practical criteria like financial feasibility, market potential, and required commitment. We will help you evaluate each entry route through this lens, narrowing down the choices based on their fit with your circumstances. Included in the Resources is an Excel spreadsheet for this purpose.

Finally, this chapter will guide you through the process of making a definitive choice, providing guidance to finalize your decision and plan the next steps. Whether your goal is to start fresh, take over an existing business, or benefit from the stability of a franchise, our goal is to ensure your choice is well-informed and aligned with both your business and personal goals.

Aligning the Decision with Personal Goals

Aligning your business decision with personal goals is key to long-term success and fulfillment. It's not just about making money—it's about ensuring that the business path you choose fits well with your lifestyle, values, and aspirations.

Now that you've worked through the action plan outlined in Chapter 1 and adjusted it through subsequent chapters, it's time to bring everything together and make the final alignment between your personal goals and business entry decisions.

Risk Tolerance

Start by revisiting your risk tolerance. This was the first step in the action plan, where you assessed your comfort with potential setbacks and your ability to manage uncertainty. By now, you should have a better understanding of how your chosen business entry path aligns with your risk tolerance. If you find that starting a new business exposes you to more financial risk than you're comfortable with, consider whether buying an existing business or opting for a franchise would be a better fit. Franchises offer a proven model with more predictable outcomes, reducing the uncertainties involved. Use your current risk tolerance assessment to decide if the level of risk matches your goals or if adjustments are needed.

Emotional Considerations

Next, reflect on emotional considerations. Both your personality and circumstances influence your ability to take on the challenges of business ownership. Revisit the emotional elements you've considered so far: how do you feel about uncertainty? Do you thrive on challenges, or do you prefer a sense of stability? If you're someone who values independence and creative freedom, starting your own business may be a better choice. On the other hand, if emotional stability and reduced stress are top priorities, buying an existing business could provide the structure and predictability you need. Remember the lessons from Chapter 5, where case studies highlighted how different emotional profiles led to varying levels of satisfaction and success. Be honest about what type of environment you need to thrive and align your decision accordingly.

Entry Costs

Entry costs and available capital are other crucial factors that need to be aligned with your goals. Throughout Chapters 2 to 4, you evaluated the costs of starting, buying, and franchising. Now, compare these financial requirements with your resources. If you're considering starting a new venture, do you have enough capital to sustain operations until the business becomes profitable? If not, are you comfortable raising external funds? Buying an existing business might require a substantial upfront investment, but it provides a more immediate cash flow compared to starting from scratch. The key is to ensure that your financial capacity and the associated costs of each option match your risk tolerance and long-term financial goals.

Your Preferred Path

With a better grasp of your risk tolerance, emotional readiness, and financial situation, it's time to identify your preferred path. If you've leaned towards starting your own business, make sure this aligns with both your risk tolerance and available resources. Likewise, if buying a business or a franchise feels like the safer choice, confirm that it aligns with your lifestyle and emotional considerations. Remember, there's no "right" answer—what's right is what fits your circumstances. Be open to adjusting your plan if something doesn't feel quite right.

To bring further alignment, consider your values and lifestyle preferences. Ask yourself if the type of business you are considering fits into your daily life. For instance, do you value spending evenings with family? If so, avoid businesses that require long hours or late-night operations.

Finally, revisit the lessons learned from the case studies in Chapter 5. Each entrepreneur faced different challenges, some of which were due to a lack of alignment between their personal goals and their business decisions. Reflect on these examples as you approach your final decision. Are there potential challenges you see in your chosen path that might create misalignment with your goals? If so, make the necessary adjustments before committing.

In conclusion, aligning your business decision with personal goals is a dynamic process. By using the action plan and making adjustments based on what you have learned, you can ensure that your choice is well-suited to your risk tolerance, emotional readiness, financial capacity, and personal values. Keep refining your framework until you feel confident that the business path you choose aligns with your long-term vision of success, not just in terms of profitability but in terms of personal fulfillment and quality of life.

Creating a Decision-Making Framework

Now that you've gathered all the information from previous chapters, it's time to create a decision-making framework that will guide your choice of business entry. A well-designed framework helps make complex decisions manageable and allows you to evaluate each option objectively. In this section, we will discuss three practical methods for building this framework: a decision matrix, a scoring system, and a step-by-step process. Each technique will help you organize your thoughts and ensure that your final decision is aligned with your goals.

Decision Matrix

A decision matrix is a straightforward tool for comparing multiple business entry options against key criteria. On one axis of the matrix, list all possible business entry methods—starting a new business, buying an existing one, or purchasing a franchise. Then, list your decision criteria along the other axis. These criteria might include risk tolerance, financial requirements, lifestyle fit, and alignment with personal values.

Assign a score to each criterion for every business entry option. Use a scale from 1 to 10, with 1 indicating poor alignment and 10 indicating excellent alignment. For example, if you value autonomy, starting a new business may receive a high score, while buying a franchise might score lower.

Once you have rated each option against all criteria, calculate the total score for each business entry method. This total will help you determine which option best aligns with your personal goals and circumstances.

The advantage of the decision matrix is that it provides a clear and objective way to assess multiple factors simultaneously. It also allows you to see trade-offs between options. For example, you might find that one business model has a higher total score but lacks in an area that is particularly important to you. Use the matrix to help discussions with partners or mentors who can help evaluate the results. Adjust based on their input and refine the framework until it reflects your priorities accurately.

Scoring System

Another practical way to create a decision-making framework is by using a scoring system. This method is similar to the decision matrix but adds weight to specific criteria based on their importance.

Start by assigning a weight to each criterion according to its significance. For instance, if risk tolerance is your top priority, you might assign it a weight of 30%, while financial readiness might be weighted at 20%.

Next, score each business entry option on a scale from 1 to 5 for each factor. Multiply each score by the weight assigned to that factor. For example, if you scored a business option as 4 for risk tolerance (weighted at 30%), its weighted score for that criterion would be 1.2 (4 x 0.3). Sum the weighted scores for each option to figure out which has the highest total.

The benefit of a scoring system is that it allows you to emphasize specific areas that matter most. This ensures that your final decision aligns closely with your priorities. It is beneficial when there are criteria of differing importance, helping you make a well-balanced choice. Keep in mind that while scoring helps prioritize options, the final decision should also consider qualitative factors, such as intuition and passion for the business idea.

Step-by-Step Process

A step-by-step process is a more structured approach that walks you through each phase of making the decision. This process involves breaking down the decision into smaller, manageable steps and evaluating each one before moving to the next. Start by revisiting your action plan from Chapter 1 and update it to reflect everything you've learned.

Step 1: Revisit Your GoalsBegin by clearly restating your personal and business goals. Consider your desired work-life balance, financial goals, and long-term vision for success. This step ensures that every subsequent decision is consistent with your broader aspirations.

Step 2: Clarify Your ConstraintsIdentify your constraints, such as available capital, risk tolerance, and time commitments. Think back to Chapters 2 to 4, where we explored entry costs and risk levels. Write down what you are willing and not willing to compromise on. This will narrow your options and prevent you from considering paths that do not align with your limits.

Step 3: Evaluate Each PathEvaluate each potential business entry path against your goals and constraints. At this stage, both qualitative and quantitative information gathered from earlier exercises will be used. Consider real-life examples from Chapter 5, where we learned about entrepreneurs who chose different paths. Apply those lessons to your situation and figure out whether any of those stories resonate with your circumstances.

Choosing the Best Method

Each of these methods—decision matrix, scoring system, and step-by-step process—offers a unique way to evaluate your options. Choosing the best one depends on your personal preference and the complexity of the decision you need to make.

Suppose you value objectivity and prefer seeing all factors laid out clearly; a decision matrix may be best. If you have specific criteria that are significantly more important than others, the scoring system will provide better clarity. Finally, if you need a structured and comprehensive approach, the step-by-step process will guide you through every aspect of the decision.

Whichever method you choose, the goal is to create a framework that aligns with your goals, values, and unique circumstances, ensuring that your decision is informed, well-reasoned, and practical.

Finalizing Your Choice

Now that you have worked through the earlier steps of aligning your decision with personal goals and creating a decision-making framework, it is time to finalize your choice. This stage involves taking everything you have learned and applying it in a structured manner to make a well-informed and confident decision. Whether you are deciding between starting a business, buying one, or entering a franchise, the aim here is to solidify your commitment to the path that best aligns with your goals, circumstances, and aspirations.

For those who are still deciding between entry options, refer to Appendix B: Resources. You will find an Excel spreadsheet named "Business Scoring Model" that can be particularly helpful. This model includes a scoring system with a list of 22 criteria to help you score each business entry option.

By using the scoring system, you can objectively evaluate each option against critical factors such as risk tolerance, financial resources, lifestyle compatibility, and personal values. Assign a score between 1 and 10 for each criterion and use the weighting system to reflect the importance of each factor to your individual goals. This will provide a numerical score that can help you compare and decide which business entry method is the most suitable.

Suppose you have already decided on a business entry path but need to compare specific businesses within that choice. In that case, the Excel spreadsheet also includes a scoring model with 15 criteria for evaluating different businesses. This is useful if, for example, you have decided to buy an existing business and need to choose between several opportunities.

These criteria include profitability, market position, scalability, and alignment with your skills and values. Assign a score to each business for every criterion and calculate the weighted total to figure out which business is the best fit.

In addition to using the scoring system, it's essential to validate your decision against your personal goals and emotional readiness. Revisit the insights gathered throughout Chapters 1 to 6, particularly the lessons learned from the case studies. Validating your decision ensures that your choice is not only practical but also fulfilling on a personal level.

Consider seeking external validation for your choice before committing. Discuss your decision with those closest to you – your family. After that, discuss your decision with a mentor, business advisor, or someone you trust who has experience in the industry. They can provide valuable feedback and identify potential blind spots. External validation not only boosts your confidence but also ensures that your decision is well-rounded and takes multiple perspectives into account.

Lastly, embrace flexibility in your approach. While finalizing your decision is a significant milestone, remain open to adjusting as added information becomes available. Market conditions, financial situations, or personal circumstances may change, and being adaptable is critical to long-term success. A finalized decision does not mean rigidity; it means having a clear direction while being ready to pivot if necessary.

Chapter Recap

In this chapter, we've combined all the concepts and tools necessary to guide you in making your final business entry decision. You've learned how to align your choice with personal goals, including lifestyle compatibility. The focus was on ensuring that the path you choose not only offers business potential but also fits harmoniously with your personal aspirations.

We discussed practical frameworks for evaluating each option, such as the decision matrix, scoring system, and step-by-step process. These frameworks were designed to simplify complex decisions and ensure that you make an informed choice. By using the scoring model in Appendix B, you can objectively evaluate different business entry options or compare specific businesses based on carefully chosen criteria.

The ultimate step is to commit to your decision. Validate your choice with trusted advisors and outline the following steps to implement it. Remain flexible, adapting if circumstances change. Your decision is a significant milestone, but success requires both commitment and adaptability.

Action Plan

Decide on the method you want to use and complete the exercise.

Please review the Business Scoring Model in Appendix B, which can assist with deciding about entry options and different business opportunities.

Discuss your findings and decisions with family members and trusted advisors.

Chapter 7
Conclusion

"There are times when delaying a decision has benefit. Often, allowing a set period of time to mull something over so your brain can work it through generates a thoughtful and effective decision"– Nancy Morris

Recap of Key Topics

In this book, we explored the different paths to entering the business world. Each chapter presented unique insights and practical advice to help you make an informed choice.

In Chapter 1, we discussed the primary business entry methods. These include starting a new business, buying an existing one, and investing in a franchise. We examined the pros and cons of each option, focusing on control, risks, and initial investment.

Chapter 2 explored the process of starting a new business. We covered essential steps such as idea generation, feasibility testing, and creating a business plan. Starting a business requires careful planning and a willingness to manage financial and operational uncertainties.

In Chapter 3, we explored buying an existing business. This path offers established customer bases, systems, and immediate cash flow. However, it comes with higher upfront costs and the risk of inheriting problems.

Chapter 4 focused on franchising. Franchising provides brand recognition, training, and support. However, the model also involves high fees and less control over operations. Selecting the right franchise is crucial for success.

Chapter 5 presented case studies. We reviewed real-life examples of entrepreneurs who started or bought businesses. These case studies revealed practical lessons in adaptability, risk management, and decision-making.

Finally, in Chapter 6, we discuss the decision-making process. We integrated all options and provided a framework, including a business scoring model, for aligning your choice with personal goals, risk tolerance, and available capital.

Final Thoughts and Encouragement

As you stand at the crossroads of starting, buying, or franchising a business, remember that no decision is flawless. Every path comes with its own set of challenges and opportunities.

Your ability to face uncertainties with a clear mind and a determined spirit will be crucial. The lessons in this book should be seen as flexible instructions and a guide to help you navigate your unique journey. Use the tools you've gained to assess risks, measure your readiness, and align your choices with your values and goals.

Business ownership demands resilience. Whether you choose to start from scratch, buy an existing company, or invest in a franchise, there will be hurdles. These hurdles may range from market shifts to personal setbacks. The important thing is to prepare, adapt, and move forward despite the obstacles. Reflect on the case studies shared here—they show that even successful entrepreneurs face moments of doubt. But they also reveal that persistence, creativity, and a commitment to growth often lead to success.

At this stage, it's natural to feel excitement mixed with apprehension. The key is to take calculated action. Don't let the fear of failure hold you back from pursuing what truly resonates with you. There will be moments that test your resolve, but every step will bring you closer to your vision. Trust in your ability to learn, grow, and overcome each challenge. Remember, there is no perfect moment to begin—action creates progress.

Your entrepreneurial journey is not just about profit; it is about growth, learning, and making an impact. Celebrate the small wins, learn from setbacks, and always keep your end goal in mind. You now have the tools, knowledge, and strategies to take that leap. Whether you start, buy, or franchise, make sure it aligns with what you truly desire.

Believe in yourself and know that you have the strength to make your business a success. Your determination will shape your future. Embrace the journey, and let each step bring you closer to the life you envision.

Next Steps

Now that you have completed this book, it's time to take action. The journey ahead requires a clear plan, courage, and a commitment to ongoing learning. The first step is to finalize your decision-making framework. Use the insights and tools provided in each chapter, including the action plan and decision-making exercises, to refine your path. Be objective and consider discussing your findings with trusted family members or advisors for added perspective.

Once you've decided on your preferred business entry option, start by setting achievable short-term goals. Break down the larger goals into smaller, manageable tasks. For example, if you decide to start a business, begin with the basics, like market research and validating your idea. If buying a business is your choice, start contacting brokers and researching potential opportunities. Those choosing franchising should evaluate franchise options based on their personal alignment and financial capabilities.

Keep reviewing and adjusting your action plan as you move forward. Flexibility is crucial, as you will face new challenges and opportunities that may require you to adapt. Don't hesitate to revisit your risk tolerance and emotional readiness at different stages.

Finally, remember that entrepreneurship is a marathon, not a sprint. Take time to celebrate each milestone, no matter how small. Stay focused, stay flexible, and continue to build on the foundation you've created with this book. Your success will come from a combination of preparation, action, and perseverance.

May your journey ahead be filled with success and fulfillment.

Afterword

Thank you for reading!

If you found this book helpful, I'd greatly appreciate it if you could take a moment to leave a review on Amazon. Your feedback not only helps me improve but also assists other readers in finding the right resources. Scan the QR code (or click on it) to share your thoughts.

I appreciate your support!

Appendix A: Action Plan

Combining the various chapters' plans, you can use this plan to help you plot your way.

Preliminary Framework

Assess Your Risk Tolerance: Reflect on your ability to manage potential setbacks. Evaluate your finances to decide how much risk you can tolerate. Consider your personal and professional goals – determining the importance of these goals compared to other life goals can help clarify your risk tolerance.

Evaluate Emotional Considerations: Consider how your personality and external circumstances, such as financial stability and family obligations, affect your ability to take on a new business venture. Decide whether you thrive on uncertainty or prefer more stability.

Analyze Entry Costs: Assess your available capital and how long you can sustain the business before it becomes profitable. Include your ability to raise external funds.

Identify Your Preferred Path: Based on your risk tolerance, emotional readiness, and financial resources, decide whether starting or buying a business is the best option for you. Also consider the franchise option.

Create a Preliminary Framework: Based on your current

understanding, develop a basic framework for your decision. Remember, this is not a final decision but rather a set of guiding parameters to refine as you gather more detailed information in the coming chapters. Stay flexible and be ready to adjust your plan as you dive deeper into the specifics of starting or buying a business.

Review and Adjust Your Preliminary Framework

After each of Chapters 2 to 4, review and adjust your preliminary framework as you progress towards a final decision.

After Chapter 5, adjust your framework according to the lessons learned and common pitfalls discussed in this chapter.

Create a Decision-Making Framework

After Chapter 6, decide on the method you want to use and complete the exercise.

Review the Business Scoring Model in Appendix B that can assist with a decision about entry options as well as different business opportunities.

Discuss your findings and decision with family members and trusted advisors.

Appendix B: Resources

These resources can be accessed by scanning or clicking the QR code, or link. Alternatively, you can download them directly from our website at www.impisimedia.com/resources, simply use the password **SBSB2**

These resources cover many pages, below is the table of contents.

1. Business Plan Framework
2. Due Diligence Investigation (DDI) checklist
3. Business valuation workbook
4. Business valuation overview
5. Business scoring model
6. Franchise Associations

1. Business Plan Framework

Scan or click this code to download your Business Plan Framework document.

Introduction

This document offers a structured approach to completing your business plan. Entrepreneurs are often at different stages of developing their business ideas—some may have a near-finished plan, while others are just starting to conceptualize. By including as much relevant information as possible, you'll provide potential partners, financiers, or investors with a clearer picture of where you stand and what support might be necessary.

The framework includes notes and questions designed to guide you through each section, helping refine your plan as you go. These notes should be deleted and replaced with your specific business details. (And this introduction can be deleted).

Keep in mind that not every section will apply to your venture, and irrelevant parts should be removed. However, be careful not to remove sections or headings simply because they are difficult or incomplete—those challenges may be essential to address before the plan is considered complete.

Basic information

Name of business
Physical address
Postal address
Contact person
Contact detail (mobile, e-mail & website if applicable)

1. Business Description

1.1 Background

History – Is this a new or existing business? If new, explain how the opportunity was identified. If existing, when was it established, what products and/or services are currently offered, where is it located, what is the revenue/turnover, how many employees, and are financial records available? This is a short and sharp summary only.

Goals – Explain the reason(s) why this business opportunity is being pursued.

1.2 Core activities of the proposed business

Describe the primary business activity.

1.3 Location

Discuss the physical location of the proposed business in terms of region, city/town, and infrastructure (roads, communications, etc.), as well as distances from the nearest main centers.

1.4 Product and/or service description

Detailed description – What products and/or services will be manufactured or sold? Use categories if applicable. Describe the income streams related to different products/services.

What is your value offering?

Typical client behavior – What products or services are potential clients currently using to fill the identified need?

Expected change – Will potential clients change from existing products to your products and why? What is required to convince them?

1.5 Ownership structure

Legal structure – Type of legal entity, legal name and registration number, trading name.

Owners – List the owners/ partners/ members/ shareholders, their shareholding, and describe their role in the business.

Contribution – What will each owner/ partner/ member/ shareholder contribute (cash, experience, contacts, time, etc.) to the business?

1.6 Legal considerations

Statutory/legal requirements – Are you aware of any legal requirements to start and operate the proposed business? (legal entity registration, tax registrations, customs and excise registrations, etc.)

Permits and or licenses – What are required? Have they been secured? If not, how far are they from completion?

Environmental impact assessment

Agreements – If a partnership or a private company with multiple members/ shareholders, does a partnership/ member/ shareholders agreement exist? Are there other crucial agreements that must be finalized? If so, give details.

2. Opportunity

2.1 Client description

If institutions or businesses, describe the typical type, size, and location. If individuals or households, describe the potential client in terms of demographics.

2.2 Geographical area where the product or service will be offered

Describe the geographical area that you will service – country, region, town? Why did you choose this area?

2.3 Market potential

Potential client base – How many potential clients are there in the geographical area that you intend to operate?

Typical spending on product/ service – What are the clients currently spending on comparable products or services to satisfy the need?

Target Clients – Based on the potential client base, what portion or segment do you realistically expect to target?

2.4 Competition

Name your competitors (direct and indirect) and discuss the following for each: competitors' core business or business activities, location, the geographical areas of operation, track record and successes, marketing methods, strengths and weaknesses.

2.5 Competitive advantage

State why your proposed business will succeed, what will make it different or better than its competitors? What is your USP?

2.6 SWOT analysis

Objectively discuss your proposed business's strengths, weaknesses, opportunities, and threats.

Discuss the barriers to entry.

3. Marketing

3.1 Costing and pricing

Cost price – How much will the products/services cost your business? Total cost includes direct cost from the suppliers and all other costs up to the point where it reaches your premises (consider the costs associated with shipping, freight, taxes).

Method of pricing – What is the estimated selling price and how was it calculated? How does the profit margin compare to industry norms?

3.2 Sales projections

Route(s) to market – Discuss the routes to market in detail, including the sequence in which they will be established.

Unit sales – Explain how many units are expected to be sold per month and why you think that it is realistic. If unit sales are not relevant, use monetary value for the projections.

Increase in sales – How do you expect sales to increase over the short and long term?

3.3 Marketing plan

Explain your branding strategy.

Explain your marketing plan, including specific actions you will employ to achieve the expected sales. Here are a few possibilities: Advertising, promotion, display, content marketing, social media marketing, public relations, representatives, event marketing, loyalty program, sponsorships.

Discuss the marketing budget and the allocation to each of these.

4. Management

4.1 The entrepreneur(s)

Discuss each owner/ partner/ member/ shareholder's background based on work history, previous business experience and knowledge, and technical expertise and knowledge of the product or services you intend to offer.

4.2 Key operational functions

Describe how the business and its various departments will

function. Depending on the type of business and its complexity, you should include Operations, Finance, Marketing, Human Resources, IT, and Admin.

Manufacturing is essentially part of Operations, but if it is a manufacturing concern, describe the manufacturing process in detail, including the steps, technical process(es), time taken, skills required, quality control, certifications, etc.

The supply chain requires special attention. For each existing and potential supplier give its name and describe location, experience and reputation, and name alternative suppliers. Discuss any agreements with suppliers, for example: Have you agreed on purchase prices and if so, what are the prices? What guarantees does the supplier offer for the products? What is the delivery schedule? What training can the supplier make available?

4.3 Personnel

Discuss the entire personnel contingent with emphasis on key personnel – Name(s) of person responsible for each function/ department (key personnel), work history and experience of key personnel, names and job descriptions of remainder of personnel.

Include an organogram.

5. Finance

5.1 Financial projections

Attach the following for the first 3 years:

– Monthly cash flow statements
– Income statements
– Balance sheets

Explain what the cash position of the business will be, how much cash it will require before it reaches breakeven and how long it will take.

5.2 Finance required

Description	Equity	Long term loans	Short term loans	Total
Start-up costs				
Land & buildings				
Plant & equipment				
Office furniture				
Vehicles				
Working capital				
Total				
Contribution	%	%	%	100%

Summarize the amount of finance required using a table like the example above, or something similar. Give full details on the source of funds as well as its application.

Explain all assumptions used and contingency plans included in the figures.

6. Supporting Documentation

Attach any document that you feel could be useful to motivate any argument or that can contribute towards a better understanding of the business proposal such as copies of permits, contracts and/or agreements already finalized.

If this is an existing business, attach financial statements for the last 3 years and management accounts not older than 3 months.

2. Due Diligence Investigation (DDI) checklist

Scan or click this code to download your DDI checklist document.

Introduction

This document offers a structured approach for the DDI. Attention to detail will help you to form a clear picture of where you stand and what further investigations might be necessary.

The framework includes the core question (shown as a Q:) that each section needs to answer, and notes designed to guide you through each section.

Keep in mind that not every section and every note will apply to your investigation, and you should delete irrelevant parts (and this introduction can also be deleted). Furthermore, you can include any note you deem necessary to develop a checklist fit for your specific circumstances. However, be careful not to remove sections or headings simply because they are difficult to investigate—those challenges may be essential to address before the DDI is complete.

General information

Registered name and number
Trading name
Postal address
Physical address
Contact person
Contact detail (mobile, e-mail, website)

Business description

Background information (Q: main reason for selling?)

– Clear understanding of how business evolved to this point and the reason for selling.

Core activity (Q: what is the primary activity?)
– Clear description of core activity(ies).

Location (Q: is the location suitable?)
– Full description.
– Overview of infrastructure, present and future.
– Distances to key places and entities.

Product and/or service description (Q: what is the product/service range?)
– Exact description of all products and services, and categories/departments if applicable.
– Copy of price list, and brochures.
– What is existing client behavior?
– What are potential clients using at present to fill their needs?
– How do these competing products/services compare?
– Why would clients change/benefit?
– Clients' willingness to pay? Clients' ability to pay?
– What is the pay-back period of the product (where applicable)?

Ownership structure (Q: who owns this business and how?)
– In what legal form does the business trade?
– List all partners /members/ shareholders and % shareholding.
– Detail of any legal entities as shareholders.
– Each shareholder's contribution, both monetary and in kind.
– Which shareholders are actively full-time involved in the business?
– Cross-check with operations and personnel section.
– Background of the non-active shareholders.
– Does a partnership/ members/ shareholders agreement exist? Copy.

Legal considerations (Q: is the business compliant and in good standing?)
– Copy of legal entity documents.
– What other registration requirements are applicable? Copies.
– Company income taxes in order? Copies.
– Other statutory registrations required? Copies.
– Any specific product/ service-related permits/licenses required? Copies.
– Lease agreement on business premises. Copy.
– Check for parties involved, property description, term, rent, levies and other costs, escalation, renewal.
– Any present litigation for or against business/owners?
– Are seller(s) willing to sign a constraint of trade or non-compete agreement?

Opportunity

Client description (Q: exactly who is the client?)
– Can clients be categorized?
– Can the demographics be described?
– Cross-check with product/service description section.
– If a single or few corporate clients, to what extent will personal influence play a role?

Geographical area of operation (Q: where does it operate?)
– Confirm all areas. Cross-check with the client description section.
– How will the product be distributed?
– Is the area subject to peculiar seasonal or other fluctuations?

Client base (Q: how healthy is the client base?)
– Check entire client list against sales, sales trend, returns, payment terms, arrears.
– Check for growth in client numbers.
– Check for sales spread amongst clients.

– Check for single clients that contribute 10% or more of revenue.

– How stable are these clients?

– What is the estimated market share?

Competition (Q: who/what are you up against?)

– For each competitor get information/ evidence of the following: Name, exact location, product/ service range, price range, area of operation, distribution methods, marketing methods, suppliers, sales or market share.

– Cross-check with client description section and area of operation section.

– Are there any emerging competitors or disruptive technologies that could impact this market segment in the next 2-5 years?

Competitive advantage (Q: what makes this business different?)

– What is the competitive advantage of the product/service?

– What is the competitive advantage of the enterprise?

– Is there a proprietary advantage? Patents? Trademarks?

– Are there barriers to entry?

– Do the explanations correlate with the client's description?

Marketing

Costing and pricing (Q: can the profit margin be confirmed?)

– How is cost price(s) calculated?

– Does it include all costs to reflect the "landed cost"?

– How is selling price(s) calculated?

– How does it compare to the competition?

– Cross-check with the competition section.

– Cross-check with the spending patterns section.

– Cross-check with other similar businesses and industry norms.

– Is there room for improvement of profit margin?

– What circumstances would force profit margins downwards?

– How likely is this scenario?

Sales projections (Q: can sales be motivated?)
– Check historic sales trends, in units as well as monetary value.
– Can fluctuations/anomalies be explained?
– Are monthly sales projections available?
– Units as well as monetary value?
– Cross-check with client potential section and competition section.
– Capacity – cross check all capacity aspects in relation to sales projections, including procurement, storage, manufacturing, delivery.

Marketing strategy and plan (Q: is the current marketing strategy adequate?)
– Does the business have a clear marketing strategy?
– Does it have a marketing plan?
– Is it practical?
– Is it cost effective?
– Does it fit the client's description?
– How does it compare to the competition?
– Are marketing actions planned in sufficient detail?
– Are these actions costed and budgeted for?

Management

Management team (Q: who and of what caliber is the team?)
– Full names and identity number (copy identity document).
– Qualifications. Work history (dates, employer, position).
– Interview the entire management team. Summarize expertise and strong/weak points.
– Clarify credit check issues if any.
– Check team chemistry.
– Check retention strategy.
– Does the management team have a succession plan in place?
– What are the contingencies if key management personnel leave?

– Are non-competition or 'restraint of trade agreements' in place?
– Check for family relationships amongst the management team.

Key operational functions (Q: how does this business function?)

– Are the various functions clearly described?
– Does it make business sense?
– How does it compare to similar businesses?
– Is each function properly planned and managed?
– Full list of personnel (name, position, salary)
– What training programs are in place/planned?
– Is the complete transaction cycle documented?
– Are there sufficient systems, procedures and internal controls to manage each function?
– Are these documented?
– Does the accounting function work smoothly?
– Is risk management addressed, specifically credit risk and risks related to key assets?
– How are cash and stock controlled?
– What management and financial reports are generated and used?
– Ensure all software and IT systems have the proper licenses and are compliant with any contractual obligations.
– Floor plan and product workflow.
– Are Health and Safety policies/procedures covered?
– If a manufacturing concern, ensure the entire manufacturing process is documented and managed properly.

Suppliers (Q: is the supply chain secure?)

– List all suppliers, for capex and stock items.
– Cross-check list of suppliers with products/services section.
– Where are suppliers located?

– What is their history?

– Are there contractual agreements?

– What are delivery/transport schedules?

– What are the different lead times?

– What are the terms for each?

– What are the guarantees?

– Do they offer training or other assistance?

– How concentrated is the supply chain?

– What is the risk if a key supplier discontinues service or raises prices significantly?

– What plans are in place for alternative suppliers?

– What is the worst-case scenario?

– Copies of supplier price lists, letters of intent, contracts.

– Random check of invoices and statements.

Environment Management System (EMS) (Q: is the EMS practical yet sufficient?)

– Does the business comply with local environmental laws and regulations?

– Does the business have an Aspect and Impact (A&I) register?

– Does the company have acceptable and realistic corrective/ proactive objectives and targets regarding significant impacts?

Finance

Financial statements (Q: what is the current financial position?)

– Are financial statements available? Are they up to date? Are they audited?

– Are management accounts available? Are they at most 3 months old?

– Is there any evidence of manipulation to avoid tax (sales/use tax, GST/HST, VAT)?

– Cross-check with tax returns.

– Are bank statements available? Inspect for any abnormal

amount and/or transaction?

– Does the business use more than one bank account? If so, why?

– Are projected financial statements or budgets available? If not, why not?

– Do historic figures and projected figures correlate? Can trends be motivated?

Revenue (Q: is revenue growth sustainable?)

– Check sales by year and month and look for trends.

– Check sales mix by product/service and department and look for trends.

– Are seasonal fluctuations identified?

– Cross-check with client records.

– Is the estimated growth in revenue realistic?

Profit margin (Q: is the theoretical profit margin achieved?)

– Check profit margin per income statements against earlier costing and pricing.

– Check net profit by year and month and look for trends.

Operating costs (Q: are costs managed properly?)

– Are expenses sufficiently detailed?

– Check each expense item against history, random invoice/statement, look for trends.

– Is owners/ partners/ members/ shareholders' remuneration reasonable?

– Cross-check labor expense with personnel section.

– Cross-check marketing expense with marketing plan section.

– Are current and forecasted expenses in line with current and forecasted revenue?

– Is there room for improvement?

Balance sheet (Q: is the snapshot of the business accurate?)

– Check all sources of funds, short and long-term, and confirm accuracy with statements.

– Check owner/member/shareholder loan accounts for significant changes.

– Are there any off-balance-sheet liabilities, such as guarantees or contingent liabilities, that might affect the business's financial standing?

– For each asset, check if it was recorded accurately, and determine how it is checked/audited and adjusted annually.

– Is depreciation applied correctly?

– Check cash/bank figures against statements.

Documents and/or tasks outstanding

_____

_____

_____

_____

_____

_____

_____

3. Business valuation workbook

This is an Excel document that can be downloaded from the website with the QR code.

Scan or click this code to download your Excel file.

4. Business valuation overview

Scan or click this code to download your Business Valuation Overview document.

Introduction

This valuation method simplifies the process and gives readers and users a practical tool for valuing a business.

Please keep in mind that this is aimed at small businesses, not large and stable corporations with long profit histories or publicly traded companies.

The 7 factors used as inputs

1. Net profit

The average net profit PA is what the purchaser can reasonably expect to achieve. This profit is quoted before tax, interest, and owner's remuneration. Unless the business has a long and stable track record accompanied by a comprehensive business plan and possibly a profit guarantee, historic profits will be used rather than projected profits.

2. Fixed assets

After compiling a list of the fixed assets that will form part of the sale, the owner needs to determine the market value of these assets. Not the book value, not the replacement value, and not the forced sale value. Market value is the monetary amount the assets will realize in the open market without unreasonable time constraints.

3. Average inventory

The average amount of inventory required for normal business activities. If the business is overstocked, the inventory will have to be decreased to an acceptable level.

4. Goodwill factor

A factor ranging between 1 (representing 12 months) and 3 (representing 36 months). This is a subjective opinion based on the characteristics of the business, such as industry, product lines, competition, supply chain, client base, branding, USP, intellectual property, barriers to entry, and any other aspect that can influence the value. A factor higher than 3 can be used in exceptional cases.

5. Required rate of return

This is a pre-tax rate of return required by the average purchaser. The rate will vary depending on the buyer's risk appetite and the business's risk profile and could range between 20% and 50%.

6. Risk-free rate of return

This is the return on short-term government bonds. Government bonds, specifically short-term bonds, are used as a guideline. The purpose of this rate is to determine the opportunity cost or the interest that will be forfeited by buying the business instead of investing that same amount in a government bond.

7. Manager's salary

The salary that would be paid to a person managing the business in the owner's absence. Note that this is a fictitious manager and has nothing to do with the existing personnel or the involvement of the present or new owner.

The 3 valuation methods

1. Extra earnings potential (EEP)

This method calculates the business's so-called extra earnings potential and determines the value of goodwill. The value of fixed assets and stock is then added to the goodwill to determine the total value of the business.

With this method, the factors weighing the heaviest are asset value and net profit.

2. Return on investment (ROI)

In this case, the question is: How much should I invest (i.e., pay for the business) to achieve the required pre-tax rate of return?

Here, the factors weighing the heaviest are the required rate of return and net profit.

3. Payback period

The length of time it will take the purchaser to recoup the entire investment. The factors weighing the heaviest are the goodwill factor and net profit.

Average value

Once the three calculations are complete, the arithmetic average is calculated. This average value is generally an accurate representation of the business's value.

Transaction structure - Inventory

The appropriate value of inventory was determined for valuation purposes, but it is a variable value that needs to be confirmed by a physical count on the date of takeover.

Since this value is variable, it is excluded from the business value, and the purchase price offered to the seller would read "...purchase price of $xxx plus inventory...".

This way, the buyer is assured that they will only pay for the value of inventory actually received on the date of the takeover.

Transaction structure – Debtors, creditors and cash

All the values calculated earlier (the three different valuation methods and the average) are the value of the business, _including_ inventory but _excluding_ debtors, creditors, and cash reserves. The reason for this is purely practical and a prudent way to structure a transaction.

On the date of the takeover, the buyer will start afresh with the debtors' and creditors' books. At the same time, the seller collects the debts that existed prior to the takeover and pays all creditors that existed prior to the takeover. In this way, the buyer avoids the risks associated with bad debts and understated creditors.

Cash is excluded as it is nonsensical to buy some money.

Summary

This valuation method is generally accurate but can be adapted depending on the peculiar circumstances of the specific business.

From the methods and calculations, it is clear that the single most important factor is the net profit since it is prominent in all three methods.

Generally, a seller wants to use future profits for calculations as it can yield a much higher value for their business. Buyers would do well to avoid this and base their calculations on historic profits. After all, that is what you are buying, a business that is producing a sure profit.

5. Business scoring model

This is an Excel document that can be downloaded from the website with the QR code.

Scan or click this code to download your Excel file.

6. Franchise Associations

USA: https://www.franchise.org/

Canada: https://cfa.ca/

The UK: https://www.thebfa.org/

Appendix C: Glossary

These definitions are concise and intended for quick reference, rather than comprehensive explanations as found in formal investment or business finance dictionaries.

Acquisition: The process of purchasing an existing business or company to grow or expand operations.

Asset Purchase Agreement (APA): A legal agreement where the buyer buys specific assets of a business, excluding liabilities unless explicitly transferred.

Brand Recognition: The extent to which consumers can identify and recall a brand, often leading to customer loyalty and trust.

Breakeven Point: The level of sales or revenue at which a business's total revenue equals its total expenses, resulting in neither profit nor loss. After breakeven, the business begins to generate profit.

Burn Rate: The rate at which a company spends its available capital to cover operational expenses. It is a key metric to determine how long a business can sustain itself before it needs additional funding.

Cash Flow Forecast: A projection of the cash inflows and outflows of a business over a specific period. It helps in planning for liquidity needs and ensuring the business can cover its obligations.

Cash Flow: The total amount of money flowing into and out of a business, regardless of its origin or purpose.

Collateral: Assets pledged by a borrower to secure a loan, which the lender can seize if the borrower defaults on the loan.

Collateralized Loan: A loan secured by an asset, which the lender can seize if the borrower defaults.

Contingency Fund: Reserves set aside to cover unexpected expenses or financial shortfalls. Typically, it is calculated as a percentage of total startup capital to provide a safety net for unforeseen challenges.

Debt-to-Equity Ratio: Also called financial gearing, is a measure of a company's financial leverage, calculated by dividing its total liabilities by shareholders' equity. A high ratio indicates over-leverage, increasing financial risk.

Discovery Day: An event hosted by a franchisor where prospective franchisees can meet leadership, learn about the franchise, and assess if it's a good fit.

Due Diligence Investigation (DDI): A thorough investigation and assessment of a business before deciding to purchase or invest, typically involving financial, operational, and legal evaluations.

Economies of Scale: The cost advantages that a business can achieve due to an increase in size, output, or scale of operation, which typically leads to a reduction in costs per unit.

Equity Stake: Ownership in a business, represented by shares.

Exclusive Territory: A geographical area granted to a franchisee where no other franchisees of the same brand can operate.

Feasibility: The ability of a business idea to be executed.

Feasibility is determined before moving to full-scale planning.

Financial Liquidity: The ability of a business to convert assets into cash quickly to meet short-term obligations.

Fixed Costs: Business expenses that do not change with the level of goods or services produced, such as rent and salaries.

Franchise Agreement: The legal contract between the franchisor and franchisee, outlining the terms and conditions of the franchise relationship.

Franchise De-Branding: Also called de-franchising, is the process of converting a franchise location to an independent business or selling it to an unrelated third party.

Franchise Disclosure Document (FDD): A legal document provided to potential franchisees, outlining important details such as fees, obligations, and legal requirements.

Franchise Fee: The upfront payment required to gain the right to operate under a franchisor's brand and systems.

Franchise: A business model in which an individual or group is given the right to operate under an established brand and system, usually involving fees and adherence to strict operational guidelines.

Franchisee Success Rate: A measure of the success of franchisees within a system, often based on profitability, growth, and business longevity.

Goodwill: An intangible asset that represents the value of a business's reputation, customer loyalty, and other non-physical factors that contribute to its profitability.

Intrapreneurship: The act of behaving like an entrepreneur while working within a larger organization, using company resources to innovate and create new ventures.

Letter of Intent (LOI): A document outlining the buyer's interest in buying a business, often including confidentiality clauses. It is not legally binding but signifies serious intent.

Leveraging: The use of borrowed funds to acquire assets or finance operations.

Management Accounts: Internal financial reports produced regularly (usually monthly) to track the financial performance of a business. They compare actual figures with forecasts and are essential for ongoing business management.

Market Opportunity: The potential demand for a product or service in a specific market. It includes analyzing the market size, target audience and competition to determine the business's chances for success.

Marketing Fee: A contribution paid by franchisees, often as a percentage of sales, to fund national or regional advertising campaigns.

Non-compete Clause: A legal provision preventing the seller of a business from starting or joining a competing business within a specified time and geographic range.

Non-solicitation Clause: A legal agreement preventing the seller from soliciting former employees or clients after selling the business.

Operational Efficiency: The capability of a business to deliver its products or services in the most cost-effective manner without compromising on quality.

Operations Manual: A detailed guide provided by the franchisor, outlining the day-to-day processes and standards that must be followed by franchisees.

Personal Guarantee: A promise made by an individual to repay a loan in the event that the business is unable to do so.

Return on Investment (ROI): A performance measure used to evaluate the efficiency of an investment, calculated by dividing the profit gained from the investment by the initial cost of the investment.

Risk Tolerance: An individual's ability and willingness to endure the uncertainty of potential monetary loss in pursuit of higher returns.

Royalty Fee: A recurring payment made by the franchisee to the franchisor, usually calculated as a percentage of sales, in exchange for ongoing support.

Seasonal Slowdown: A predictable period of reduced business activity due to seasonal factors.

Suspensive Sale Agreement: A contract where ownership of a business is transferred to the buyer only after full payment is completed, often used in seller financing.

Sustained Growth: Long-term and consistent business expansion, characterized by increasing revenue, market share, and profitability. Sustained growth is typically achieved through strategic planning, market adaptation, and strong management practices.

Synergies: The potential financial and operational benefits gained from merging two or more companies, resulting in a value greater than the sum of the individual parts.

Transfer Fee: A fee charged by a franchisor when a franchise is sold or transferred to a new owner.

Valuation Method: Techniques used to determine the financial value of a business, often based on its net profit, assets, and market position.

Variable Costs: Costs that vary with production output, such as raw materials and commission-based wages.

Viability: The long-term sustainability and profitability of a business, reflecting its ability to survive and thrive in its market after it has been established.

Working Capital: The funds necessary to cover the day-to-day operational expenses of a business until it reaches profitability. It includes cash needed for rent, salaries, supplies, and other ongoing costs.

About the Author

Born in South Africa and now residing in Panama, Charlie Victor has dedicated his life to the world of small business. With a Bachelor of Commerce and a postgraduate degree in Investment Management, he has a solid academic foundation that complements his practical experience. A serial entrepreneur, Charlie has spent his entire career immersed in small business finance, development and management.

After serving as a pilot in the military, he turned his focus to the business world, assisting hundreds of small businesses in their growth journeys. Many of these ventures have flourished into large, profitable enterprises. Before taking early retirement, Charlie co-founded and served as COO of an international SME finance company where he played a pivotal role in establishing and training in-country teams.

With extensive travel experience, much of it work-related, Charlie draws on his extensive experiences to provide practical, actionable advice for prospective entrepreneurs and new small business owners.

About the Publisher

Impisi™ Media is a dynamic publishing company dedicated to creating and distributing high-quality intellectual property, including books, e-books, audiobooks, and journals.

Our content is crafted to inform, inspire, and empower a global audience. Our commitment to innovation and excellence drives us to deliver content that resonates and adds value to our readers and listeners.

Visit our website https://impisimedia.com

facebook.com/impisimedia

instagram.com/impisimedia

pinterest.com/impisimedia

www.ingramcontent.com/pod-product-compliance
Lightning Source LLC
Chambersburg PA
CBHW071227210326

41597CB00016B/1974